# Syllable Savvy Spelling

**Syl$^{3}$ la$^{2}$ ble$^{3}$**

**Sav$^{3}$ vy$^{2}$**

**Spel$^{4}$ ling$^{4}$**

***A simple strategy that spells success.***

Karen K. Newell

Learn For Your Life

Third Edition 2015


Cover Design by Christy Short

Learn For Your Life Publishing
Camp Hill, PA 17011

www.Learn4YourLife.com

# *Instructor's Guide*

Welcome to Syllable Savvy Spelling. This simple technique will not only improve your students' spelling scores this year, but will provide them with a successful strategy that will improve their spelling ability for years to come. In fact, you will likely find that your own ability to spell difficult words is improved after teaching this technique.

## THREE COLUMN APPROACH

You will notice that each lesson has three columns. The first is the Phonetic Column. This allows the student to sound out the word using the common dictionary symbols for each phonetic sound. The second column displays the word as it is usually written. The third column is the Syllable Column and prints the words in syllables and gives the number of letters in each syllable. This column prompts the student to focus on the syllables in each word, and the specific letters in the syllables.

### Phonetic Column

The Phonetic Column gives the dictionary symbols to allow the student to sound out the word. This has two benefits. First, the student can practice the words each day without having the answer right in plain view simply by folding the lesson page so only the first column is showing. As an alternative to folding the paper, another sheet of paper can be placed over the second and third columns. Second, seeing only the phonetic column allows the student to work independently, rather than have a teacher or partner dictate the word without them seeing it.

The symbols used in Syllable Savvy are common symbols used in dictionaries. The exception is the short vowel sound. This is the sound one would hear preceding a "ck" at the end of the word (ie. back, deck, sick, lock, duck). In many dictionaries, the short sound is marked with a curved line, somewhat like a smile, over the letter. In Syllable Savvy, the short vowel sound has no symbol. The long vowel sound is marked with the standard flat line over the vowel. (ie, bāke, mē, līke, hōpe, tūne)

At the bottom of each lesson page, is a quick pronunciation key which lists the sounds indicated by the different marks. Apart from the short and long vowel sounds, it is not necessary for the student to attempt to memorize any of the other marks. Of course, they will get much more familiar with these marks by using Syllable Savvy Spelling.

One other sound should be mentioned, which is the schwa sound, indicated by the symbol which looks like an upside down e. This is the vowel sound in the non-stressed syllables which rhymes with "duh." It may be spelled with an "a", "e", "i", o," u", or "y".

The pronunciation marks provided are based on one common pronunciation for the word. Some words have different pronunciations, many of which are regional. If the pronunciation listed is different than that used in your home, you have three options. One, the word on the lesson may be erased with white out, and the familiar pronunciation substituted. Or, the more familiar pronunciation can be written above the one on the lesson page, emphasizing to the students that there is more than one correct way to pronounce a word. Finally, one can acknowledge the differences with the student and leave the word as it is. Probably, it is best to use whatever approach is preferred by the student.

Spelling texts for fifth grade and above

also have the stressed syllables underlined. It should be noted that some words represent more than one part of speech and the pronunciation may be different. For instance, "content" as a noun has the first syllable stressed. "Content" as an adjective as the second syllable stressed. Most of the time we have used the pronunciation for the noun form since it is generally more common.

PHONETIC COLUMN:
A WARNING

It should be noted that some younger children in lower grades may have difficulty with the Phonetic Column. It may be confusing to some students when they are presented with the "wrong" letters and the phonetic marks may reinforce using the wrong letters. Of course, the purpose of Syllable Savvy is to promote correct spelling, and if a student finds the phonetic "clues" confusing, this is counter-productive. However, other aspects of Syllable Savvy can still be used. If you determine the phonetic marks are confusing to your student, you may choose not to emphasize the Phonetic Column. In several more months, or even a year, the student may be ready to sound out the word from the phonetic spelling.

If you chose not to use the Phonetic Column for a younger child, there are a few techniques that could be employed to keep the benefit of the phonetic clues. First, a picture or sample sentence can be written on one side of an index card, and the other two columns written on the opposite side. For instance, if the spelling word is "ocean", the first side could have the sentence, "Let's go swim in the o......" and have the waves of the sea drawn on the card. The opposite side of the card could list the regular spelling and the Syllable Column.

Another technique to allow the student to work independently on their spelling list without seeing the word each time they practice it; is to record the word and a sentence using the word with a tape player or computer. The student can listen to hear the spoken word and then write the word on paper.

Of course, the old fashioned way of having a parent or partner read the words on the list to the student can still be used. One of the values of Syllable Savvy Spelling is that it allows the student to study all of the words independently. Some younger students, however, are not necessarily ready for that independence and do better working with someone else.

**Middle Column**

The middle column displays the word with its standard spelling. This is the way the students will encounter the word and in most cases they will be familiar with it. It is obvious that it is much easier to read a familiar word than it is to spell it.

**Syllable Column**

The Syllable Column breaks each word into its syllables. This is the natural way to write complex words. It also has the advantage of giving the students syllables that are usually only two to four letters long. That is much less intimidating than facing a long word with what appears to be an unattainable number of letters.

After each syllable, the number of letters in that syllable is displayed in superscript. This helps the student to focus on the specific letters in each syllable.

The number at the end of the syllable also aids the students in correcting their own work. Often students will look at a longer word they have just written and think it looks "about right" and not compare each letter on their list and the master list. Day after day, this reinforces writing the word incorrectly. By writing the word in syllables, then recording how many letters they correctly wrote in each syllable, the student receives immediate feedback. It also becomes more obvious to them if one letter is incorrect.

## FIVE EXTRA SPACES

Each lesson consists of 20 words. However, only 15 words are listed on the Lesson Page. This is because it is important to include in the students' study of spelling those words that are particularly important for them. These words can include words they misspelled from previous spelling lessons, words they misspell in their creative writing, or words that are part of their science, social studies, or other unit studies.

## ONE LESSON PER WEEK

Each Syllable Savvy Spelling level consists of thirty weekly lessons. Each lesson consists of four pages. The fifth day of the week is the spelling test.

You will notice that each lesson is printed two times with two sets of blank lines on the opposing pages. This is so the students have the Phonetic Column in front of them as they do their exercises. They will use the first page for Days 1 and 2, then turn to the second page for Days 3 and 4.

## HOW IT WORKS

### 1st Day

The first day of the lesson, the student will first encounter the new spelling words. This is most effective if it is done one-on-one with the instructor. After the first day, the student will practice the words independently. Of course, some older students prefer to work independently, and once they have been taught the steps below, they may prefer to do even the first day's work on their own.

1. Look at the spelling word in the middle column. For most of the words in this program, the word will be familiar to the students. Read the word together.
2. Look at the pronunciation of the word in the first column or Phonetic Column. Help the student sound the word out using the pronunciation key at the bottom of the page.
3. Look at each syllable in the Syllable Column. Ask, "Is this the way you would expect this syllable to be written? Is there anything tricky or difficult here?" Thankfully, most syllables aren't too difficult.
4. Any letters that are not expected can be underlined with a colored pencil. This is an optional step; but some students find that the focus required to identify the unexpected letters helps to cement them in their memory.
5. Cover the middle and third columns so they are not visible. Then the student will write the word on the correct line on the opposing page. They should write it in syllables with breaks between each syllable.
6. After the entire word is written, the student will look at the Syllable Column again to correct the word. The student checks the number of letters in each syllable as recorded in the Syllable Column with the letters they actually wrote on their page. If the letters are all correct, the student moves to the next syllable.
7. Syllable by syllable the student checks

the letters they have written with the word on the Syllable Column.

8. If all syllables in the word were written correctly, color in the box at the end of the line. That gives a small but tangible pat ont he back for their good work.
9. Next move to the next word on the spelling list.
10. If any part of the word was missed, it needs to be written again on a separate sheet of paper. Focus specific attention on the syllable(s) missed.
11. Any missed letters can be underlined on the Syllable Column of the lesson. This will flag the student to note those letters while doing their daily review.

HOW IT WORKS

2nd - 4th Days

On the second, third, and fourth days of the week, the student will practice writing their words using the same technique. Even if they worked with the teacher the first day, they will do these practice sessions alone.

Students begin by reviewing the first page of the lesson. Any unusual spellings or difficult words have been marked on this page previously.

Then students will either fold the page to show only the Phonetic Column, or cover the second two columns with another sheet of the paper. They then proceed to write the words in the column marked for that day. Words are written syllable by syllable as before.

Before proceeding to the next word, students self-correct the word they just wrote. They verify every letter in every syllable. At the end of each syllable, they write the number of correct letters. If all letters in a word are correct, they indicate the word was written correctly by coloring in the box.

Incorrect words must be rewritten on a separate page. They need to write each word until every syllable is written correctly

ALTERNATIVE

As an alternative to writing in the book, a student can fold a regular piece of lined writing paper in half the long way. That makes two columns on each side, or four total for the front and back. They can use the same paper for one week. They can cover the second and third columns with their writing paper as they proceed down the page.

SPELLING TEST

5th Day

The last day of the week, the spelling test is given. The teacher dictates each word and the student writes it on a separate sheet of paper.

GRADING

Usually, with a twenty word spelling list, each word is worth five points. Therefore, the grade to the test can be determined by multiplying the number of incorrect words on the test by five, and subtracting the product from 100 percent.

The daily practices can be graded and counted as quiz grades for students who need additional help in spelling. On a quiz, each syllable can be counted as two points. Therefore, a student is getting partial credit for the syllables they write correctly. The words written on the first day are not included as a quiz grade, as the student is encountering the word for the first time. The three quiz grades can be averaged. The quiz grades can be equal to one test grade.

An alternative method is to give one bonus point for each daily practice page. This gives credit to the student for keeping on track and making progress through the week.

## SPELLING RULES

You will notice that many of the words have tiny chalk boards with a single letter on it. This letter refers to the appropriate rule in the Spelling Rules index in the back of the book.

We have two goals with these Spelling Rules. First, we want to show common rules which will assist student's spelling ability without having them memorize every possible rule in the English language. The point is not to memorize rules, but to group common spelling patterns so they are easier to remember.

Second, an occasional review of the spelling rules will cement the pattern in their mind as well as the correct spelling of words they have learned. You might consider giving a monthly spot quiz to see if they can spell words from one or two rules.

Many students find it helpful to keep a list of words with a common pattern. This is a great technique in teaching phonics in kindergarten through second grade, but can be continued with spelling patterns in older grades as well. Students may like to write the words directly on the Spelling Rules page, or keep a separate notebook.

## TEACHING TIPS

It takes discipline for a student to develop the habit of sounding out each syllable phonetically while writing the letters simultaneously. Therefore, it takes effort on your part to coach them in developing that skill. It is an effort well worth your time that will pay off for both of you.

On the first day, as the child is writing the weekly list for the first time, listen that he or she verbalizes each syllable as it is written. If they do not, ask them to rewrite it while speaking it. Occasionally during the week you can also listen and remind them to develop this habit.

Visual learners often find that highlighting the vowels with a yellow highlighter helps them to remember them. Some have found that using a different colored highlighter for different vowel combinations is helpful. However, there are only a few colors of highlighters so this may not be as useful unless you also keep a variety of colored markers on hand as well.

Kinetic learners who like motion or touch can write their words in the air, draw them on a velvet covered board, or spell them in cursive with their toes. Young dancers particularly like that last technique.

Keeping a notebook of common spelling patterns is useful for younger students. However, even older students find it helpful for certain patterns such as "ough" or "sion." As an alternative to a notebook, use the Spelling Rules pages or the extra pages at the end of the book as a place to write hard to remember words. A quick review once a month will enable students to remember words previously learned and connect them to new ones as they are presented.

*Syllable Savvy Spelling Six*

| Day 1 | | Day 2 | |
|---|---|---|---|
| 1. ______ | ☐ | 1. ______ | ☐ |
| 2. ______ | ☐ | 2. ______ | ☐ |
| 3. ______ | ☐ | 3. ______ | ☐ |
| 4. ______ | ☐ | 4. ______ | ☐ |
| 5. ______ | ☐ | 5. ______ | ☐ |
| 6. ______ | ☐ | 6. ______ | ☐ |
| 7. ______ | ☐ | 7. ______ | ☐ |
| 8. ______ | ☐ | 8. ______ | ☐ |
| 9. ______ | ☐ | 9. ______ | ☐ |
| 10. ______ | ☐ | 10. ______ | ☐ |
| 11. ______ | ☐ | 11. ______ | ☐ |
| 12. ______ | ☐ | 12. ______ | ☐ |
| 13. ______ | ☐ | 13. ______ | ☐ |
| 14. ______ | ☐ | 14. ______ | ☐ |
| 15. ______ | ☐ | 15. ______ | ☐ |
| 16. ______ | ☐ | 16. ______ | ☐ |
| 17. ______ | ☐ | 17. ______ | ☐ |
| 18. ______ | ☐ | 18. ______ | ☐ |
| 19. ______ | ☐ | 19. ______ | ☐ |
| 20. ______ | ☐ | 20. ______ | ☐ |

| **ā** | **âr** | **är** | **er** | **ē** | **ēr** | **ī** | **ō** | **ŏŏ** | **ôr** | **ow** | **oy** | **ū** | **zh** | **ə** |
|---|---|---|---|---|---|---|---|---|---|---|---|---|---|---|
| day | air | far | her | bee | tear | light | rope | book | for | cow | boy | tune | vision | item |

# Lesson 1

| | | | |
|---|---|---|---|
| 1. | is rē əl | Israel | Is$^{2}$ ra$^{2}$ el$^{2}$ |
| 2. | jə rū sə ləm | Jerusalem | Je$^{2}$ ru$^{2}$ sa$^{2}$ lem$^{3}$ |
| 3. | le bə non | Lebanon | Leb$^{3}$ a$^{1}$ non$^{3}$ |
| 4. | bā rūt | Beirut | Bei$^{3}$ rut$^{3}$ |
| 5. | ser prīz | surprise | sur$^{3}$ prise$^{5}$ |
| 6. | fūl ish nis | foolishness | fool$^{4}$ ish$^{3}$ ness$^{4}$ |
| 7. | per fikt | perfect | per$^{3}$ fect$^{4}$ |
| 8. | sel ə brāt | celebrate | cel$^{3}$ e$^{1}$ brate$^{5}$ |
| 9. | pop ū lā shn | population | pop$^{3}$ u$^{1}$ la$^{2}$ tion$^{4}$ |
| 10. | ol thō | although | al$^{2}$ though$^{6}$ |
| 11. | gâr ən tē | guarantee | guar$^{4}$ an$^{2}$ tee$^{3}$ |
| 12. | fo lō ēn | following | fol$^{3}$ low$^{3}$ ing$^{3}$ |
| 13. | ges | guess | guess$^{5}$ |
| 14. | rē sôrs | resource | re$^{2}$ source$^{6}$ |
| 15. | con sə qwins | consequence | con$^{3}$ se$^{2}$ quence$^{6}$ |
| 16. | | | |
| 17. | | | |
| 18. | | | |
| 19. | | | |
| 20. | | | |

L

O

| ā | âr | är | er | ē | ēr | ī | ō | ŏŏ | ôr | ow | oy | ū | zh | ə |
|---|---|---|---|---|---|---|---|---|---|---|---|---|---|---|
| day | air | far | her | bee | tear | light | rope | book | for | cow | boy | tune | vision | item |

Day 3

1. ______________________ ☐
2. ______________________ ☐
3. ______________________ ☐
4. ______________________ ☐
5. ______________________ ☐
6. ______________________ ☐
7. ______________________ ☐
8. ______________________ ☐
9. ______________________ ☐
10. ______________________ ☐
11. ______________________ ☐
12. ______________________ ☐
13. ______________________ ☐
14. ______________________ ☐
15. ______________________ ☐
16. ______________________ ☐
17. ______________________ ☐
18. ______________________ ☐
19. ______________________ ☐
20. ______________________ ☐

Day 4

1. ______________________ ☐
2. ______________________ ☐
3. ______________________ ☐
4. ______________________ ☐
5. ______________________ ☐
6. ______________________ ☐
7. ______________________ ☐
8. ______________________ ☐
9. ______________________ ☐
10. ______________________ ☐
11. ______________________ ☐
12. ______________________ ☐
13. ______________________ ☐
14. ______________________ ☐
15. ______________________ ☐
16. ______________________ ☐
17. ______________________ ☐
18. ______________________ ☐
19. ______________________ ☐
20. ______________________ ☐

| ā | âr | är | er | ē | ēr | ī | ō | ŏŏ | ôr | ow | oy | ū | zh | ə |
|---|---|---|---|---|---|---|---|---|---|---|---|---|---|---|
| day | air | far | her | bee | tear | light | rope | book | for | cow | boy | tune | vision | item |

# Lesson 1b

| | | | |
|---|---|---|---|
| 1. | is rē əl | Israel | Is[2] ra[2] el[2] |
| 2. | jə rū sə ləm | Jerusalem | Je[2] ru[2] sa[2] lem[3] |
| 3. | le bə non | Lebanon | Leb[3] a[1] non[3] |
| 4. | bā rūt | Beirut | Bei[3] rut[3] |
| 5. | ser prīz | surprise | sur[3] prise[5] |
| 6. | fūl ish nis | foolishness | fool[4] ish[3] ness[4] |
| 7. | per fikt | perfect | per[3] fect[4] |
| 8. | sel ə brāt | celebrate | cel[3] e[1] brate[5] |
| 9. | pop ū lā shn | population | pop[3] u[1] la[2] tion[4] |
| 10. | ol thō | although | al[2] though[6] |
| 11. | gâr ən tē | guarantee | guar[4] an[2] tee[3] |
| 12. | fo lō ēn | following | fol[3] low[3] ing[3] |
| 13. | ges | guess | guess[5] |
| 14. | rē sôrs | resource | re[2] source[6] |
| 15. | con sə qwins | consequence | con[3] se[2] quence[6] |
| 16. | | | |
| 17. | | | |
| 18. | | | |
| 19. | | | |
| 20. | | | |

| ā | âr | är | er | ē | ēr | ī | ō | ŏŏ | ôr | ow | oy | ū | zh | ə |
|---|---|---|---|---|---|---|---|---|---|---|---|---|---|---|
| day | air | far | her | bee | tear | light | rope | book | for | cow | boy | tune | vision | item |

*Syllable Savvy Spelling Six*

| Day 1 | | Day 2 | |
|---|---|---|---|
| **1.** | ☐ | **1.** | ☐ |
| **2.** | ☐ | **2.** | ☐ |
| **3.** | ☐ | **3.** | ☐ |
| **4.** | ☐ | **4.** | ☐ |
| **5.** | ☐ | **5.** | ☐ |
| **6.** | ☐ | **6.** | ☐ |
| **7.** | ☐ | **7.** | ☐ |
| **8.** | ☐ | **8.** | ☐ |
| **9.** | ☐ | **9.** | ☐ |
| **10.** | ☐ | **10.** | ☐ |
| **11.** | ☐ | **11.** | ☐ |
| **12.** | ☐ | **12.** | ☐ |
| **13.** | ☐ | **13.** | ☐ |
| **14.** | ☐ | **14.** | ☐ |
| **15.** | ☐ | **15.** | ☐ |
| **16.** | ☐ | **16.** | ☐ |
| **17.** | ☐ | **17.** | ☐ |
| **18.** | ☐ | **18.** | ☐ |
| **19.** | ☐ | **19.** | ☐ |
| **20.** | ☐ | **20.** | ☐ |

| **ā** | **âr** | **är** | **er** | **ē** | **ēr** | **ī** | **ō** | **ŏŏ** | **ôr** | **ow** | **oy** | **ū** | **zh** | **ə** |
|---|---|---|---|---|---|---|---|---|---|---|---|---|---|---|
| day | air | far | her | bee | tear | light | rope | book | for | cow | boy | tune | vision | item |

# Lesson 2

| | | | | |
|---|---|---|---|---|
| 1. | sēr ē ə | Syria | Syr$^3$ i$^1$ a$^1$ | |
| 2. | də mas kəs | Damascus | Da$^2$ mas$^3$ cus$^3$ | |
| 3. | i rok | Iraq | Ir$^2$ aq$^2$ | |
| 4. | bag dad | Baghdad | Bagh$^4$ dad$^3$ | |
| 5. | kom ə kāt | complicate | com$^3$ pli$^3$ cate$^4$ | |
| 6. | per fer ā shn | perforation | per$^3$ for$^3$ a$^1$ tion$^4$ | |
| 7. | də mē ner | demeanor | de$^2$ mea$^3$ nor$^3$ | Q |
| 8. | hek tik | hectic | hec$^3$ tic$^3$ | |
| 9. | o ner | honor | hon$^3$ or$^2$ | Q |
| 10. | lo ji kl | logical | log$^3$ i$^1$ cal$^3$ | |
| 11. | sher lē | surely | sure$^4$ ly$^2$ | |
| 12. | pil ler | pillar | pil$^3$ lar$^3$ | R |
| 13. | rā zin | raisin | rai$^3$ sin$^3$ | |
| 14. | märvd | carved | carv$^4$ed$^2$ | J |
| 15. | rū tēn | routine | rou$^3$ tine$^4$ | |
| 16. | | | | |
| 17. | | | | |
| 18. | | | | |
| 19. | | | | |
| 20. | | | | |

| ā | âr | är | er | ē | ēr | ī | ō | ŏŏ | ôr | ow | oy | ū | zh | ə |
|---|---|---|---|---|---|---|---|---|---|---|---|---|---|---|
| day | air | far | her | bee | tear | light | rope | book | for | cow | boy | tune | vision | item |

## Day 3

1. ____________ ☐
2. ____________ ☐
3. ____________ ☐
4. ____________ ☐
5. ____________ ☐
6. ____________ ☐
7. ____________ ☐
8. ____________ ☐
9. ____________ ☐
10. ____________ ☐
11. ____________ ☐
12. ____________ ☐
13. ____________ ☐
14. ____________ ☐
15. ____________ ☐
16. ____________ ☐
17. ____________ ☐
18. ____________ ☐
19. ____________ ☐
20. ____________ ☐

## Day 4

1. ____________ ☐
2. ____________ ☐
3. ____________ ☐
4. ____________ ☐
5. ____________ ☐
6. ____________ ☐
7. ____________ ☐
8. ____________ ☐
9. ____________ ☐
10. ____________ ☐
11. ____________ ☐
12. ____________ ☐
13. ____________ ☐
14. ____________ ☐
15. ____________ ☐
16. ____________ ☐
17. ____________ ☐
18. ____________ ☐
19. ____________ ☐
20. ____________ ☐

| **ā** | **âr** | **är** | **er** | **ē** | **ēr** | **ī** | **ō** | **ŏŏ** | **ôr** | **ow** | **oy** | **ū** | **zh** | **ə** |
|---|---|---|---|---|---|---|---|---|---|---|---|---|---|---|
| day | air | far | her | bee | tear | light | rope | book | for | cow | boy | tune | vision | item |

# Lesson 2b

| | | | |
|---|---|---|---|
| 1. | sēr ē ə | Syria | Syr$^3$ i$^1$ a$^1$ |
| 2. | də mas kəs | Damascus | Da$^2$ mas$^3$ cus$^3$ |
| 3. | i rok | Iraq | Ir$^2$ aq$^2$ |
| 4. | bag dad | Baghdad | Bagh$^4$ dad$^3$ |
| 5. | kom ə kāt | complicate | com$^3$ pli$^3$ cate$^4$ |
| 6. | per fer ā shn | perforation | per$^3$ for$^3$ a$^1$ tion$^4$ |
| 7. | də mē ner | demeanor | de$^2$ mea$^3$ nor$^3$ |
| 8. | hek tik | hectic | hec$^3$ tic$^3$ |
| 9. | o ner | honor | hon$^3$ or$^2$ |
| 10. | lo ji kl | logical | log$^3$ i$^1$ cal$^3$ |
| 11. | sher lē | surely | sure$^4$ ly$^2$ |
| 12. | pil ler | pillar | pil$^3$ lar$^3$ |
| 13. | rā zin | raisin | rai$^3$ sin$^3$ |
| 14. | cärvd | carved | carv$^4$ed$^2$ |
| 15. | rū tēn | routine | rou$^3$ tine$^4$ |
| 16. | | | |
| 17. | | | |
| 18. | | | |
| 19. | | | |
| 20. | | | |

| ā | âr | är | er | ē | ēr | ī | ō | ŏŏ | ôr | ow | oy | ū | zh | ə |
|---|---|---|---|---|---|---|---|---|---|---|---|---|---|---|
| day | air | far | her | bee | tear | light | rope | book | for | cow | boy | tune | vision | item |

*Syllable Savvy Spelling Six*

| Day 1 | | Day 2 | |
|---|---|---|---|
| 1. | ☐ | 1. | ☐ |
| 2. | ☐ | 2. | ☐ |
| 3. | ☐ | 3. | ☐ |
| 4. | ☐ | 4. | ☐ |
| 5. | ☐ | 5. | ☐ |
| 6. | ☐ | 6. | ☐ |
| 7. | ☐ | 7. | ☐ |
| 8. | ☐ | 8. | ☐ |
| 9. | ☐ | 9. | ☐ |
| 10. | ☐ | 10. | ☐ |
| 11. | ☐ | 11. | ☐ |
| 12. | ☐ | 12. | ☐ |
| 13. | ☐ | 13. | ☐ |
| 14. | ☐ | 14. | ☐ |
| 15. | ☐ | 15. | ☐ |
| 16. | ☐ | 16. | ☐ |
| 17. | ☐ | 17. | ☐ |
| 18. | ☐ | 18. | ☐ |
| 19. | ☐ | 19. | ☐ |
| 20. | ☐ | 20. | ☐ |

| ā | âr | är | er | ē | ēr | ī | ō | ŏŏ | ôr | ow | oy | ū | zh | ə |
|---|---|---|---|---|---|---|---|---|---|---|---|---|---|---|
| day | air | far | her | bee | tear | light | rope | book | for | cow | boy | tune | vision | item |

# Lesson 3

| | | | | |
|---|---|---|---|---|
| 1. | so dē ə rā bē ə | Saudi Arabia | Sau$^{3}$ di$^{2}$ A$^{1}$ ra$^{2}$ bi$^{2}$ a$^{1}$ | |
| 2. | rē od | Riyadh | Riy$^{3}$ adh$^{3}$ | |
| 3. | i ron | Iran | Ir$^{2}$ an$^{2}$ | |
| 4. | ter on | Tehran | Teh$^{3}$ ran$^{3}$ | |
| 5. | ver chū | virtue | vir$^{3}$ tue$^{3}$ | |
| 6. | ver chū əs | virtuous | vir$^{3}$ tu$^{2}$ ous$^{3}$ | T |
| 7. | grēv | grieve | grieve$^{6}$ | S |
| 8. | rē sēv | receive | re$^{2}$ ceive$^{5}$ | S |
| 9. | im pos ə bl | impossible | im$^{2}$ pos$^{3}$ si$^{2}$ ble$^{3}$ | |
| 10. | sil ə bl | syllable | syl$^{3}$ la$^{2}$ ble$^{3}$ | |
| 11. | eks pīr | expire | ex$^{2}$ pire$^{4}$ | |
| 12. | eks per ā shn | expiration | ex$^{2}$ pir$^{3}$ a$^{1}$ tion$^{4}$ | |
| 13. | a pə tīt | appetite | ap$^{2}$ pe$^{2}$ tite$^{4}$ | |
| 14. | tres pa sēn | trespassing | tres$^{4}$ pas$^{3}$ sing$^{4}$ | K |
| 15. | op shn | option | op$^{2}$ tion$^{4}$ | |
| 16. | | | | |
| 17. | | | | |
| 18. | | | | |
| 19. | | | | |
| 20. | | | | |

| ā | âr | är | er | ē | ēr | ī | ō | ŏŏ | ôr | ow | oy | ū | zh | ə |
|---|---|---|---|---|---|---|---|---|---|---|---|---|---|---|
| day | air | far | her | bee | tear | light | rope | book | for | cow | boy | tune | vision | item |

| Day 3 | | Day 4 | |
|---|---|---|---|
| 1. ______ | ☐ | 1. ______ | ☐ |
| 2. ______ | ☐ | 2. ______ | ☐ |
| 3. ______ | ☐ | 3. ______ | ☐ |
| 4. ______ | ☐ | 4. ______ | ☐ |
| 5. ______ | ☐ | 5. ______ | ☐ |
| 6. ______ | ☐ | 6. ______ | ☐ |
| 7. ______ | ☐ | 7. ______ | ☐ |
| 8. ______ | ☐ | 8. ______ | ☐ |
| 9. ______ | ☐ | 9. ______ | ☐ |
| 10. ______ | ☐ | 10. ______ | ☐ |
| 11. ______ | ☐ | 11. ______ | ☐ |
| 12. ______ | ☐ | 12. ______ | ☐ |
| 13. ______ | ☐ | 13. ______ | ☐ |
| 14. ______ | ☐ | 14. ______ | ☐ |
| 15. ______ | ☐ | 15. ______ | ☐ |
| 16. ______ | ☐ | 16. ______ | ☐ |
| 17. ______ | ☐ | 17. ______ | ☐ |
| 18. ______ | ☐ | 18. ______ | ☐ |
| 19. ______ | ☐ | 19. ______ | ☐ |
| 20. ______ | ☐ | 20. ______ | ☐ |

| ā | âr | är | er | ē | ēr | ī | ō | ŏŏ | ôr | ow | oy | ū | zh | ə |
|---|---|---|---|---|---|---|---|---|---|---|---|---|---|---|
| day | air | far | her | bee | tear | light | rope | book | for | cow | boy | tune | vision | item |

# Lesson 3b

| | | | |
|---|---|---|---|
| 1. | so dē ə rā bē ə | Saudi Arabia | Sau$^3$ di$^2$ A$^1$ ra$^2$ bi$^2$ a$^1$ |
| 2. | rē od | Riyadh | Riy$^3$ adh$^3$ |
| 3. | i ron | Iran | Ir$^2$ an$^2$ |
| 4. | ter on | Tehran | Teh$^3$ ran$^3$ |
| 5. | ver chū | virtue | vir$^3$ tue$^3$ |
| 6. | ver chū əs | virtuous | vir$^3$ tu$^2$ ous$^3$ |
| 7. | grēv | grieve | grieve$^6$ |
| 8. | rē sēv | receive | re$^2$ ceive$^5$ |
| 9. | im pos ə bl | impossible | im$^2$ pos$^3$ si$^2$ ble$^3$ |
| 10. | sil ə bl | syllable | syl$^3$ la$^2$ ble$^3$ |
| 11. | eks pīr | expire | ex$^2$ pire$^4$ |
| 12. | eks per ā shn | expiration | ex$^2$ pir$^3$ a$^1$ tion$^4$ |
| 13. | a pə tīt | appetite | ap$^2$ pe$^2$ tite$^4$ |
| 14. | tres pa sēn | trespassing | tres$^4$ pas$^3$ sing$^4$ |
| 15. | op shn | option | op$^2$ tion$^4$ |
| 16. | | | |
| 17. | | | |
| 18. | | | |
| 19. | | | |
| 20. | | | |

| ā | âr | är | er | ē | ēr | ī | ō | ŏŏ | ôr | ow | oy | ū | zh | ə |
|---|---|---|---|---|---|---|---|---|---|---|---|---|---|---|
| day | air | far | her | bee | tear | light | rope | book | for | cow | boy | tune | vision | item |

Syllable Savvy Spelling Six

| Day 1 | | Day 2 | |
|---|---|---|---|
| 1. | ☐ | 1. | ☐ |
| 2. | ☐ | 2. | ☐ |
| 3. | ☐ | 3. | ☐ |
| 4. | ☐ | 4. | ☐ |
| 5. | ☐ | 5. | ☐ |
| 6. | ☐ | 6. | ☐ |
| 7. | ☐ | 7. | ☐ |
| 8. | ☐ | 8. | ☐ |
| 9. | ☐ | 9. | ☐ |
| 10. | ☐ | 10. | ☐ |
| 11. | ☐ | 11. | ☐ |
| 12. | ☐ | 12. | ☐ |
| 13. | ☐ | 13. | ☐ |
| 14. | ☐ | 14. | ☐ |
| 15. | ☐ | 15. | ☐ |
| 16. | ☐ | 16. | ☐ |
| 17. | ☐ | 17. | ☐ |
| 18. | ☐ | 18. | ☐ |
| 19. | ☐ | 19. | ☐ |
| 20. | ☐ | 20. | ☐ |

| **ā** | **âr** | **är** | **er** | **ē** | **ēr** | **ī** | **ō** | **ŏŏ** | **ôr** | **ow** | **oy** | **ū** | **zh** | **ə** |
|---|---|---|---|---|---|---|---|---|---|---|---|---|---|---|
| day | air | far | her | bee | tear | light | rope | book | for | cow | boy | tune | vision | item |

# Lesson 4

| | | | |
|---|---|---|---|
| 1. | af gan i stan | Afghanistan | Af$^{2}$ ghan$^{4}$ is$^{2}$ tan$^{3}$ |
| 2. | ku bəl | Kabul | Ka$^{2}$ bul$^{3}$ |
| 3. | pak i stan | Pakistan | Pak$^{3}$ is$^{2}$ tan$^{3}$ |
| 4. | is lom ə bad | Islamabad | Is$^{2}$ lam$^{3}$ a$^{1}$ bad$^{3}$ |
| 5. | sim fən ē | symphony | sym$^{3}$ phon$^{4}$ y$^{1}$ |
| 6. | ôr kis trə | orchestra | or$^{2}$ che$^{3}$ stra$^{4}$ |
| 7. | pē a nō | piano | pi$^{2}$ a$^{1}$ no$^{2}$ |
| 8. | gi tär | guitar | gui$^{3}$ tar$^{3}$ |
| 9. | bās | bass | bass$^{4}$ |
| 10. | tre bl | treble | tre$^{3}$ ble$^{3}$ |
| 11. | per ku shn | percussion | per$^{3}$ cus$^{3}$ sion$^{4}$ |
| 12. | zī lə fōn | xylophone | xy$^{2}$ lo$^{2}$ phone$^{5}$ |
| 13. | chel ō | cello | cel$^{3}$ lo$^{2}$ |
| 14. | vī ō lin | violin | vi$^{2}$ o$^{1}$ lin$^{3}$ |
| 15. | trom bōn | trombone | trom$^{4}$ bone$^{4}$ |
| 16. | | | |
| 17. | | | |
| 18. | | | |
| 19. | | | |
| 20. | | | |

M

R

| ā | âr | är | er | ē | ēr | ī | ō | ŏŏ | ôr | ow | oy | ū | zh | ə |
|---|---|---|---|---|---|---|---|---|---|---|---|---|---|---|
| day | air | far | her | bee | tear | light | rope | book | for | cow | boy | tune | vision | item |

*Syllable Savvy Spelling Six*

## Day 3

1. ______________ ☐
2. ______________ ☐
3. ______________ ☐
4. ______________ ☐
5. ______________ ☐
6. ______________ ☐
7. ______________ ☐
8. ______________ ☐
9. ______________ ☐
10. ______________ ☐
11. ______________ ☐
12. ______________ ☐
13. ______________ ☐
14. ______________ ☐
15. ______________ ☐
16. ______________ ☐
17. ______________ ☐
18. ______________ ☐
19. ______________ ☐
20. ______________ ☐

## Day 4

1. ______________ ☐
2. ______________ ☐
3. ______________ ☐
4. ______________ ☐
5. ______________ ☐
6. ______________ ☐
7. ______________ ☐
8. ______________ ☐
9. ______________ ☐
10. ______________ ☐
11. ______________ ☐
12. ______________ ☐
13. ______________ ☐
14. ______________ ☐
15. ______________ ☐
16. ______________ ☐
17. ______________ ☐
18. ______________ ☐
19. ______________ ☐
20. ______________ ☐

| **ā** | **âr** | **är** | **er** | **ē** | **ēr** | **ī** | **ō** | **ŏŏ** | **ôr** | **ow** | **oy** | **ū** | **zh** | **ə** |
|---|---|---|---|---|---|---|---|---|---|---|---|---|---|---|
| day | air | far | her | bee | tear | light | rope | book | for | cow | boy | tune | vision | item |

# Lesson 4b

| | | | |
|---|---|---|---|
| 1. | af gan i stan | Afghanistan | Af$^{2}$ ghan$^{4}$ is$^{2}$ tan$^{3}$ |
| 2. | ku bəl | Kabul | Ka$^{2}$ bul$^{3}$ |
| 3. | pak i stan | Pakistan | Pak$^{3}$ is$^{2}$ tan$^{3}$ |
| 4. | is lom ə bad | Islamabad | Is$^{2}$ lam$^{3}$ a$^{1}$ bad$^{3}$ |
| 5. | sim fən ē | symphony | sym$^{3}$ phon$^{4}$ y$^{1}$ |
| 6. | ôr kis trə | orchestra | or$^{2}$ che$^{3}$ stra$^{4}$ |
| 7. | pē a nō | piano | pi$^{2}$ a$^{1}$ no$^{2}$ |
| 8. | gi tär | guitar | gui$^{3}$ tar$^{3}$ |
| 9. | bās | bass | bass$^{4}$ |
| 10. | tre bl | treble | tre$^{3}$ ble$^{3}$ |
| 11. | per ku shn | percussion | per$^{3}$ cus$^{3}$ sion$^{4}$ |
| 12. | zī lə fōn | xylophone | xy$^{2}$ lo$^{2}$ phone$^{5}$ |
| 13. | chel ō | cello | cel$^{3}$ lo$^{2}$ |
| 14. | vī ō lin | violin | vi$^{2}$ o$^{1}$ lin$^{3}$ |
| 15. | trom bōn | trombone | trom$^{4}$ bone$^{4}$ |
| 16. | | | |
| 17. | | | |
| 18. | | | |
| 19. | | | |
| 20. | | | |

| ā | âr | är | er | ē | ēr | ī | ō | ŏŏ | ôr | ow | oy | ū | zh | ə |
|---|---|---|---|---|---|---|---|---|---|---|---|---|---|---|
| day | air | far | her | bee | tear | light | rope | book | for | cow | boy | tune | vision | item |

## Day 1

1. ______________ ☐
2. ______________ ☐
3. ______________ ☐
4. ______________ ☐
5. ______________ ☐
6. ______________ ☐
7. ______________ ☐
8. ______________ ☐
9. ______________ ☐
10. ______________ ☐
11. ______________ ☐
12. ______________ ☐
13. ______________ ☐
14. ______________ ☐
15. ______________ ☐
16. ______________ ☐
17. ______________ ☐
18. ______________ ☐
19. ______________ ☐
20. ______________ ☐

## Day 2

1. ______________ ☐
2. ______________ ☐
3. ______________ ☐
4. ______________ ☐
5. ______________ ☐
6. ______________ ☐
7. ______________ ☐
8. ______________ ☐
9. ______________ ☐
10. ______________ ☐
11. ______________ ☐
12. ______________ ☐
13. ______________ ☐
14. ______________ ☐
15. ______________ ☐
16. ______________ ☐
17. ______________ ☐
18. ______________ ☐
19. ______________ ☐
20. ______________ ☐

| **ā** | **âr** | **är** | **er** | **ē** | **ēr** | **ī** | **ō** | **ŏŏ** | **ôr** | **ow** | **oy** | **ū** | **zh** | **ə** |
|---|---|---|---|---|---|---|---|---|---|---|---|---|---|---|
| day | air | far | her | bee | tear | light | rope | book | for | cow | boy | tune | vision | item |

# Lesson 5

| | | | | |
|---|---|---|---|---|
| 1. | nôr wā | Norway | Nor$^3$ way$^3$ | |
| 2. | oz lō | Oslo | Os$^2$ lo$^2$ | |
| 3. | swē dn | Sweden | Swe$^3$ den$^3$ | |
| 4. | stok holm | Stockholm | Stock$^5$ holm$^4$ | |
| 5. | sə vēr | severe | sev$^3$ ere$^3$ | |
| 6. | prē zerv | preserve | pre$^3$ serve$^5$ | |
| 7. | per sə vēr | persevere | per$^3$ se$^2$ vere$^4$ | |
| 8. | myū zik | music | mu$^2$ sic$^3$ | |
| 9. | myū zi shn | musician | mu$^2$ si$^2$ cian$^4$ | T |
| 10. | sin the tik | synthetic | syn$^3$ the$^3$ tic$^3$ | |
| 11. | sep er āt* | separate | sep$^3$ ar$^2$ ate$^3$ | G |
| 12. | ser ownd | surround | sur$^3$ round$^5$ | |
| 13. | pre sher | pressure | pres$^4$ sure$^4$ | |
| 14. | welth | wealth | wealth$^6$ | |
| 15. | lī sins | license | li$^2$ cense$^5$ | |
| 16. | | | | |
| 17. | | | | |
| 18. | | | | |
| 19. | | | | |
| 20. | | | | |

*Read the G Rule. These words have a recommended "spelling pronunciations" due to unusual spellings.

| ā | âr | är | er | ē | ēr | ī | ō | ŏŏ | ôr | ow | oy | ū | zh | ə |
|---|---|---|---|---|---|---|---|---|---|---|---|---|---|---|
| day | air | far | her | bee | tear | light | rope | book | for | cow | boy | tune | vision | item |

Syllable Savvy Spelling Six

## Day 3

1. ______________________ ☐
2. ______________________ ☐
3. ______________________ ☐
4. ______________________ ☐
5. ______________________ ☐
6. ______________________ ☐
7. ______________________ ☐
8. ______________________ ☐
9. ______________________ ☐
10. ______________________ ☐
11. ______________________ ☐
12. ______________________ ☐
13. ______________________ ☐
14. ______________________ ☐
15. ______________________ ☐
16. ______________________ ☐
17. ______________________ ☐
18. ______________________ ☐
19. ______________________ ☐
20. ______________________ ☐

## Day 4

1. ______________________ ☐
2. ______________________ ☐
3. ______________________ ☐
4. ______________________ ☐
5. ______________________ ☐
6. ______________________ ☐
7. ______________________ ☐
8. ______________________ ☐
9. ______________________ ☐
10. ______________________ ☐
11. ______________________ ☐
12. ______________________ ☐
13. ______________________ ☐
14. ______________________ ☐
15. ______________________ ☐
16. ______________________ ☐
17. ______________________ ☐
18. ______________________ ☐
19. ______________________ ☐
20. ______________________ ☐

| ā | âr | är | er | ē | ēr | ī | ō | ŏŏ | ôr | ow | oy | ū | zh | ə |
|---|---|---|---|---|---|---|---|---|---|---|---|---|---|---|
| day | air | far | her | bee | tear | light | rope | book | for | cow | boy | tune | vision | item |

# Lesson 5b

| | | | |
|---|---|---|---|
| 1. | nôr wā | Norway | Nor$^{3}$ way$^{3}$ |
| 2. | oz lō | Oslo | Os$^{2}$ lo$^{2}$ |
| 3. | swē dn | Sweden | Swe$^{3}$ den$^{3}$ |
| 4. | stok holm | Stockholm | Stock$^{5}$ holm$^{4}$ |
| 5. | sə vēr | severe | sev$^{3}$ ere$^{3}$ |
| 6. | prē zerv | preserve | pre$^{3}$ serve$^{5}$ |
| 7. | per sə vēr | persevere | per$^{3}$ se$^{2}$ vere$^{4}$ |
| 8. | myū zik | music | mu$^{2}$ sic$^{3}$ |
| 9. | myū zi shn | musician | mu$^{2}$ si$^{2}$ cian$^{4}$ |
| 10. | sin the tik | synthetic | syn$^{3}$ the$^{3}$ tic$^{3}$ |
| 11. | sep er āt* | separate | sep$^{3}$ ar$^{2}$ ate$^{3}$ |
| 12. | ser ownd | surround | sur$^{3}$ round$^{5}$ |
| 13. | pre sher | pressure | pres$^{4}$ sure$^{4}$ |
| 14. | welth | wealth | wealth$^{6}$ |
| 15. | lī sins | license | li$^{2}$ cense$^{5}$ |
| 16. | | | |
| 17. | | | |
| 18. | | | |
| 19. | | | |
| 20. | | | |

| ā | âr | är | er | ē | ēr | ī | ō | ŏŏ | ôr | ow | oy | ū | zh | ə |
|---|---|---|---|---|---|---|---|---|---|---|---|---|---|---|
| day | air | far | her | bee | tear | light | rope | book | for | cow | boy | tune | vision | item |

| Day 1 | | Day 2 | |
|---|---|---|---|
| 1. | ☐ | 1. | ☐ |
| 2. | ☐ | 2. | ☐ |
| 3. | ☐ | 3. | ☐ |
| 4. | ☐ | 4. | ☐ |
| 5. | ☐ | 5. | ☐ |
| 6. | ☐ | 6. | ☐ |
| 7. | ☐ | 7. | ☐ |
| 8. | ☐ | 8. | ☐ |
| 9. | ☐ | 9. | ☐ |
| 10. | ☐ | 10. | ☐ |
| 11. | ☐ | 11. | ☐ |
| 12. | ☐ | 12. | ☐ |
| 13. | ☐ | 13. | ☐ |
| 14. | ☐ | 14. | ☐ |
| 15. | ☐ | 15. | ☐ |
| 16. | ☐ | 16. | ☐ |
| 17. | ☐ | 17. | ☐ |
| 18. | ☐ | 18. | ☐ |
| 19. | ☐ | 19. | ☐ |
| 20. | ☐ | 20. | ☐ |

| ā | âr | är | er | ē | ēr | ī | ō | ŏŏ | ôr | ow | oy | ū | zh | ə |
|---|---|---|---|---|---|---|---|---|---|---|---|---|---|---|
| day | air | far | her | bee | tear | light | rope | book | for | cow | boy | tune | vision | item |

# Lesson 6

| | | | | |
|---|---|---|---|---|
| 1. | den märk | Denmark | Den$^{3}$ mark$^{4}$ | |
| 2. | kō pen hā gen | Copenhagen | Co$^{2}$ pen$^{3}$ ha$^{2}$ gen$^{3}$ | |
| 3. | ī rə lənd | Ireland | Ir$^{2}$ e$^{1}$ land$^{4}$ | |
| 4. | dub lin | Dublin | Dub$^{3}$ lin$^{3}$ | |
| 5. | so səj | sausage | sau$^{3}$ sage$^{4}$ | |
| 6. | prə tek shn | protection | pro$^{3}$ tec$^{3}$ tion$^{4}$ | |
| 7. | brēf lē | briefly | brief$^{5}$ ly$^{2}$ | S |
| 8. | här mə nē | harmony | har$^{3}$ mon$^{3}$ y$^{1}$ | |
| 9. | mel ə dē | melody | mel$^{3}$ o$^{1}$ dy$^{2}$ | |
| 10. | mə rēn | marine | ma$^{2}$ rine$^{4}$ | |
| 11. | ə kwâr ē əm | aquarium | a$^{1}$ quar$^{4}$ i$^{1}$ um$^{2}$ | M |
| 12. | ō shn | ocean | o$^{1}$ cean$^{4}$ | |
| 13. | fak ter ē | factory | fac$^{3}$ tor$^{3}$ y$^{1}$ | |
| 14. | kof | cough | cough$^{5}$ | O |
| 15. | pro gres | progress | pro$^{3}$ gress$^{5}$ | |
| 16. | | | | |
| 17. | | | | |
| 18. | | | | |
| 19. | | | | |
| 20. | | | | |

| ā | âr | är | er | ē | ēr | ī | ō | ŏŏ | ôr | ow | oy | ū | zh | ə |
|---|---|---|---|---|---|---|---|---|---|---|---|---|---|---|
| day | air | far | her | bee | tear | light | rope | book | for | cow | boy | tune | vision | item |

## Day 3

1. ____________ ☐
2. ____________ ☐
3. ____________ ☐
4. ____________ ☐
5. ____________ ☐
6. ____________ ☐
7. ____________ ☐
8. ____________ ☐
9. ____________ ☐
10. ____________ ☐
11. ____________ ☐
12. ____________ ☐
13. ____________ ☐
14. ____________ ☐
15. ____________ ☐
16. ____________ ☐
17. ____________ ☐
18. ____________ ☐
19. ____________ ☐
20. ____________ ☐

## Day 4

1. ____________ ☐
2. ____________ ☐
3. ____________ ☐
4. ____________ ☐
5. ____________ ☐
6. ____________ ☐
7. ____________ ☐
8. ____________ ☐
9. ____________ ☐
10. ____________ ☐
11. ____________ ☐
12. ____________ ☐
13. ____________ ☐
14. ____________ ☐
15. ____________ ☐
16. ____________ ☐
17. ____________ ☐
18. ____________ ☐
19. ____________ ☐
20. ____________ ☐

| **ā** | **âr** | **är** | **er** | **ē** | **ēr** | **ī** | **ō** | **ŏŏ** | **ôr** | **ow** | **oy** | **ū** | **zh** | **ə** |
|---|---|---|---|---|---|---|---|---|---|---|---|---|---|---|
| day | air | far | her | bee | tear | light | rope | book | for | cow | boy | tune | vision | item |

# Lesson 6b

| | | | |
|---|---|---|---|
| 1. | den märk | Denmark | Den$^{3}$ mark$^{4}$ |
| 2. | kō pen hā gen | Copenhagen | Co$^{2}$ pen$^{3}$ ha$^{2}$ gen$^{3}$ |
| 3. | ī rə lənd | Ireland | Ir$^{2}$ e$^{1}$ land$^{4}$ |
| 4. | dub lin | Dublin | Dub$^{3}$ lin$^{3}$ |
| 5. | so səj | sausage | sau$^{3}$ sage$^{4}$ |
| 6. | prə tek shn | protection | pro$^{3}$ tec$^{3}$ tion$^{4}$ |
| 7. | brēf lē | briefly | brief$^{5}$ ly$^{2}$ |
| 8. | här mə nē | harmony | har$^{3}$ mon$^{3}$ y$^{1}$ |
| 9. | mel ə dē | melody | mel$^{3}$ o$^{1}$ dy$^{2}$ |
| 10. | mə rēn | marine | ma$^{2}$ rine$^{4}$ |
| 11. | ə kwâr ē əm | aquarium | a$^{1}$ quar$^{4}$ i$^{1}$ um$^{2}$ |
| 12. | ō shn | ocean | o$^{1}$ cean$^{4}$ |
| 13. | fak ter ē | factory | fac$^{3}$ tor$^{3}$ y$^{1}$ |
| 14. | kof | cough | cough$^{5}$ |
| 15. | pro gres | progress | pro$^{3}$ gress$^{5}$ |
| 16. | | | |
| 17. | | | |
| 18. | | | |
| 19. | | | |
| 20. | | | |

| ā | âr | är | er | ē | ēr | ī | ō | ŏŏ | ôr | ow | oy | ū | zh | ə |
|---|---|---|---|---|---|---|---|---|---|---|---|---|---|---|
| day | air | far | her | bee | tear | light | rope | book | for | cow | boy | tune | vision | item |

| Day 1 | | Day 2 | |
|---|---|---|---|
| 1. ______________ | ☐ | 1. ______________ | ☐ |
| 2. ______________ | ☐ | 2. ______________ | ☐ |
| 3. ______________ | ☐ | 3. ______________ | ☐ |
| 4. ______________ | ☐ | 4. ______________ | ☐ |
| 5. ______________ | ☐ | 5. ______________ | ☐ |
| 6. ______________ | ☐ | 6. ______________ | ☐ |
| 7. ______________ | ☐ | 7. ______________ | ☐ |
| 8. ______________ | ☐ | 8. ______________ | ☐ |
| 9. ______________ | ☐ | 9. ______________ | ☐ |
| 10. ______________ | ☐ | 10. ______________ | ☐ |
| 11. ______________ | ☐ | 11. ______________ | ☐ |
| 12. ______________ | ☐ | 12. ______________ | ☐ |
| 13. ______________ | ☐ | 13. ______________ | ☐ |
| 14. ______________ | ☐ | 14. ______________ | ☐ |
| 15. ______________ | ☐ | 15. ______________ | ☐ |
| 16. ______________ | ☐ | 16. ______________ | ☐ |
| 17. ______________ | ☐ | 17. ______________ | ☐ |
| 18. ______________ | ☐ | 18. ______________ | ☐ |
| 19. ______________ | ☐ | 19. ______________ | ☐ |
| 20. ______________ | ☐ | 20. ______________ | ☐ |

| **ā** | **âr** | **är** | **er** | **ē** | **ēr** | **ī** | **ō** | **ŏŏ** | **ôr** | **ow** | **oy** | **ū** | **zh** | **ə** |
|---|---|---|---|---|---|---|---|---|---|---|---|---|---|---|
| day | air | far | her | bee | tear | light | rope | book | for | cow | boy | tune | vision | item |

# Lesson 7

| | | | | |
|---|---|---|---|---|
| 1. | U nī tid Kēng dəm | United Kingdom | U$^{1}$ ni$^{2}$ ted$^{3}$ King$^{4}$ dom$^{3}$ | |
| 2. | Lun dən | London | Lon$^{3}$ don$^{3}$ | |
| 3. | spān | Spain | Spain$^{5}$ | |
| 4. | mə drid | Madrid | Mad$^{3}$ rid$^{3}$ | |
| 5. | ser tən | certain | cer$^{3}$ tain$^{4}$ | |
| 6. | ker tən | curtain | cur$^{3}$ tain$^{4}$ | |
| 7. | un ser tən tē | uncertainty | un$^{2}$ cer$^{3}$ tain$^{4}$ ty$^{2}$ | |
| 8. | bō gəs | bogus | bo$^{2}$ gus$^{3}$ | L |
| 9. | lo | law | law$^{3}$ | |
| 10. | prō fownd | profound | pro$^{3}$ found$^{5}$ | |
| 11. | kum pə nē | company | com$^{3}$ pa$^{3}$ ny$^{2}$ | |
| 12. | lēnd | leaned | lean$^{4}$ed$^{2}$ | J |
| 13. | si zers | scissors | scis$^{4}$ sors$^{4}$ | |
| 14. | in lärj | enlarge | en$^{2}$ large$^{5}$ | |
| 15. | rē zult | result | re$^{2}$ sult$^{4}$ | |
| 16. | | | | |
| 17. | | | | |
| 18. | | | | |
| 19. | | | | |
| 20. | | | | |

| ā | âr | är | er | ē | ēr | ī | ō | ŏŏ | ôr | ow | oy | ū | zh | ə |
|---|---|---|---|---|---|---|---|---|---|---|---|---|---|---|
| day | air | far | her | bee | tear | light | rope | book | for | cow | boy | tune | vision | item |

## Day 3

1. ______________________ ☐
2. ______________________ ☐
3. ______________________ ☐
4. ______________________ ☐
5. ______________________ ☐
6. ______________________ ☐
7. ______________________ ☐
8. ______________________ ☐
9. ______________________ ☐
10. ______________________ ☐
11. ______________________ ☐
12. ______________________ ☐
13. ______________________ ☐
14. ______________________ ☐
15. ______________________ ☐
16. ______________________ ☐
17. ______________________ ☐
18. ______________________ ☐
19. ______________________ ☐
20. ______________________ ☐

## Day 4

1. ______________________ ☐
2. ______________________ ☐
3. ______________________ ☐
4. ______________________ ☐
5. ______________________ ☐
6. ______________________ ☐
7. ______________________ ☐
8. ______________________ ☐
9. ______________________ ☐
10. ______________________ ☐
11. ______________________ ☐
12. ______________________ ☐
13. ______________________ ☐
14. ______________________ ☐
15. ______________________ ☐
16. ______________________ ☐
17. ______________________ ☐
18. ______________________ ☐
19. ______________________ ☐
20. ______________________ ☐

| ā | âr | är | er | ē | ēr | ī | ō | ŏŏ | ôr | ow | oy | ū | zh | ə |
|---|---|---|---|---|---|---|---|---|---|---|---|---|---|---|
| day | air | far | her | bee | tear | light | rope | book | for | cow | boy | tune | vision | item |

# Lesson 7b

| | | | |
|---|---|---|---|
| 1. | U nī tid Kēng dəm | United Kingdom | U$^1$ ni$^2$ ted$^3$ King$^4$ dom$^3$ |
| 2. | Lun dən | London | Lon$^3$ don$^3$ |
| 3. | spān | Spain | Spain$^5$ |
| 4. | mə drid | Madrid | Mad$^3$ rid$^3$ |
| 5. | ser tən | certain | cer$^3$ tain$^4$ |
| 6. | ker tən | curtain | cur$^3$ tain$^4$ |
| 7. | un ser tən tē | uncertainty | un$^2$ cer$^3$ tain$^4$ ty$^2$ |
| 8. | bō gəs | bogus | bo$^2$ gus$^3$ |
| 9. | lo | law | law$^3$ |
| 10. | prō fownd | profound | pro$^3$ found$^5$ |
| 11. | kum pə nē | company | com$^3$ pa$^3$ ny$^2$ |
| 12. | lēnd | leaned | lean$^4$ed$^2$ |
| 13. | si zers | scissors | scis$^4$ sors$^4$ |
| 14. | in lärj | enlarge | en$^2$ large$^5$ |
| 15. | rē zult | result | re$^2$ sult$^4$ |
| 16. | | | |
| 17. | | | |
| 18. | | | |
| 19. | | | |
| 20. | | | |

| ā | âr | är | er | ē | ēr | ī | ō | ŏŏ | ôr | ow | oy | ū | zh | ə |
|---|---|---|---|---|---|---|---|---|---|---|---|---|---|---|
| day | air | far | her | bee | tear | light | rope | book | for | cow | boy | tune | vision | item |

Syllable Savvy Spelling Six

| Day 1 | | Day 2 | |
|---|---|---|---|
| 1. | ☐ | 1. | ☐ |
| 2. | ☐ | 2. | ☐ |
| 3. | ☐ | 3. | ☐ |
| 4. | ☐ | 4. | ☐ |
| 5. | ☐ | 5. | ☐ |
| 6. | ☐ | 6. | ☐ |
| 7. | ☐ | 7. | ☐ |
| 8. | ☐ | 8. | ☐ |
| 9. | ☐ | 9. | ☐ |
| 10. | ☐ | 10. | ☐ |
| 11. | ☐ | 11. | ☐ |
| 12. | ☐ | 12. | ☐ |
| 13. | ☐ | 13. | ☐ |
| 14. | ☐ | 14. | ☐ |
| 15. | ☐ | 15. | ☐ |
| 16. | ☐ | 16. | ☐ |
| 17. | ☐ | 17. | ☐ |
| 18. | ☐ | 18. | ☐ |
| 19. | ☐ | 19. | ☐ |
| 20. | ☐ | 20. | ☐ |

| ā | âr | är | er | ē | ēr | ī | ō | ŏŏ | ôr | ow | oy | ū | zh | ə |
|---|---|---|---|---|---|---|---|---|---|---|---|---|---|---|
| day | air | far | her | bee | tear | light | rope | book | for | cow | boy | tune | vision | item |

# Lesson 8

| | | | | |
|---|---|---|---|---|
| 1. | frans | France | France$^{6}$ | |
| 2. | pâr is | Paris | Par$^{3}$ is$^{2}$ | |
| 3. | bel jum | Belgium | Bel$^{3}$ gium$^{4}$ | |
| 4. | brus əls | Brussels | Brus$^{4}$ sels$^{4}$ | |
| 5. | sə kyer | secure | se$^{2}$ cure$^{4}$ | |
| 6. | sə kyer i tē | security | se$^{2}$ cur$^{3}$ i$^{1}$ ty$^{2}$ | |
| 7. | kum pūt | compute | com$^{3}$ pute$^{4}$ | |
| 8. | kum pūt er | computer | com$^{3}$ put$^{3}$ er$^{2}$ | |
| 9. | lē gəl | legal | le$^{2}$ gal$^{3}$ | L |
| 10. | pil grim | pilgrim | pil$^{3}$ grim$^{4}$ | |
| 11. | kon sī ens* | conscience | con$^{3}$ science$^{7}$ | G |
| 12. | kon shəs | conscious | con$^{3}$ scious$^{6}$ | T |
| 13. | īs brāk er | ice breaker | ice$^{3}$ break$^{5}$ er$^{2}$ | |
| 14. | fo sit | faucet | fau$^{3}$ cet$^{3}$ | |
| 15. | plum ēn | plumbing | plumb$^{5}$ ing$^{3}$ | |
| 16. | | | | |
| 17. | | | | |
| 18. | | | | |
| 19. | | | | |
| 20. | | | | |

| ā | âr | är | er | ē | ēr | ī | ō | ŏŏ | ôr | ow | oy | ū | zh | ə |
|---|---|---|---|---|---|---|---|---|---|---|---|---|---|---|
| day | air | far | her | bee | tear | light | rope | book | for | cow | boy | tune | vision | item |

*Syllable Savvy Spelling Six*

## Day 1

1. ______________________ ☐
2. ______________________ ☐
3. ______________________ ☐
4. ______________________ ☐
5. ______________________ ☐
6. ______________________ ☐
7. ______________________ ☐
8. ______________________ ☐
9. ______________________ ☐
10. ______________________ ☐
11. ______________________ ☐
12. ______________________ ☐
13. ______________________ ☐
14. ______________________ ☐
15. ______________________ ☐
16. ______________________ ☐
17. ______________________ ☐
18. ______________________ ☐
19. ______________________ ☐
20. ______________________ ☐

## Day 2

1. ______________________ ☐
2. ______________________ ☐
3. ______________________ ☐
4. ______________________ ☐
5. ______________________ ☐
6. ______________________ ☐
7. ______________________ ☐
8. ______________________ ☐
9. ______________________ ☐
10. ______________________ ☐
11. ______________________ ☐
12. ______________________ ☐
13. ______________________ ☐
14. ______________________ ☐
15. ______________________ ☐
16. ______________________ ☐
17. ______________________ ☐
18. ______________________ ☐
19. ______________________ ☐
20. ______________________ ☐

| ā | âr | är | er | ē | ēr | ī | ō | ŏŏ | ôr | ow | oy | ū | zh | ə |
|---|---|---|---|---|---|---|---|---|---|---|---|---|---|---|
| day | air | far | her | bee | tear | light | rope | book | for | cow | boy | tune | vision | item |

# Lesson 8b

| | | | |
|---|---|---|---|
| 1. | frans | France | France[6] |
| 2. | pâr is | Paris | Par[3] is[2] |
| 3. | bel jum | Belgium | Bel[3] gium[4] |
| 4. | brus əls | Brussels | Brus[4] sels[4] |
| 5. | sə kyer | secure | se[2] cure[4] |
| 6. | sə kyer i tē | security | se[2] cur[3] i[1] ty[2] |
| 7. | kum pūt | compute | com[3] pute[4] |
| 8. | kum pūt er | computer | com[3] put[3] er[2] |
| 9. | lē gəl | legal | le[2] gal[3] |
| 10. | pil grim | pilgrim | pil[3] grim[4] |
| 11. | kon sī ens* | conscience | con[3] science[7] |
| 12. | kon shəs | conscious | con[3] scious[6] |
| 13. | īs brāk er | ice breaker | ice[3] break[5] er[2] |
| 14. | fo sit | faucet | fau[3] cet[3] |
| 15. | plum ēn | plumbing | plumb[5] ing[3] |
| 16. | | | |
| 17. | | | |
| 18. | | | |
| 19. | | | |
| 20. | | | |

| ā | âr | är | er | ē | ēr | ī | ō | ŏŏ | ôr | ow | oy | ū | zh | ə |
|---|---|---|---|---|---|---|---|---|---|---|---|---|---|---|
| day | air | far | her | bee | tear | light | rope | book | for | cow | boy | tune | vision | item |

Syllable Savvy Spelling Six

## Day 1

1. ______________ ☐
2. ______________ ☐
3. ______________ ☐
4. ______________ ☐
5. ______________ ☐
6. ______________ ☐
7. ______________ ☐
8. ______________ ☐
9. ______________ ☐
10. ______________ ☐
11. ______________ ☐
12. ______________ ☐
13. ______________ ☐
14. ______________ ☐
15. ______________ ☐
16. ______________ ☐
17. ______________ ☐
18. ______________ ☐
19. ______________ ☐
20. ______________ ☐

## Day 2

1. ______________ ☐
2. ______________ ☐
3. ______________ ☐
4. ______________ ☐
5. ______________ ☐
6. ______________ ☐
7. ______________ ☐
8. ______________ ☐
9. ______________ ☐
10. ______________ ☐
11. ______________ ☐
12. ______________ ☐
13. ______________ ☐
14. ______________ ☐
15. ______________ ☐
16. ______________ ☐
17. ______________ ☐
18. ______________ ☐
19. ______________ ☐
20. ______________ ☐

| **ā** | **âr** | **är** | **er** | **ē** | **ēr** | **ī** | **ō** | **ŏŏ** | **ôr** | **ow** | **oy** | **ū** | **zh** | **ə** |
|---|---|---|---|---|---|---|---|---|---|---|---|---|---|---|
| day | air | far | her | bee | tear | light | rope | book | for | cow | boy | tune | vision | item |

# Lesson 9

| | | | |
|---|---|---|---|
| 1. | ne ther ləndz | Netherlands | Ne$^{2}$ ther$^{4}$ lands$^{5}$ |
| 2. | am ster dam | Amsterdam | Am$^{2}$ ster$^{4}$ dam$^{3}$ |
| 3. | jer mə nē | Germany | Ger$^{3}$ man$^{3}$ y$^{1}$ |
| 4. | ber lin | Berlin | Ber$^{3}$ lin$^{3}$ |
| 5. | ad ə kwət | adequate | ad$^{2}$ e$^{1}$ quate$^{5}$ |
| 6. | kors (way or direction) | course | course$^{6}$ |
| 7. | kors (rough) | coarse | coarse$^{6}$ |
| 8. | in krēs | increase | in$^{2}$ crease$^{6}$ |
| 9. | dē krēs | decrease | de$^{2}$ crease$^{6}$ |
| 10. | a nə ver ser ē | anniversary | an$^{2}$ niv$^{3}$ er$^{2}$ sar$^{3}$ y$^{1}$ |
| 11. | pī ə nēr | pioneer | pi$^{2}$ o$^{1}$ neer$^{4}$ |
| 12. | tīp | type | type$^{4}$ |
| 13. | tip i kl | typical | typ$^{3}$ i$^{1}$ cal$^{3}$ |
| 14. | pos ə bl | possible | pos$^{3}$ si$^{2}$ ble$^{3}$ |
| 15. | pos ə blē | possibly | pos$^{3}$ si$^{2}$ bly$^{3}$ |
| 16. | | | |
| 17. | | | |
| 18. | | | |
| 19. | | | |
| 20. | | | |

| ā | âr | är | er | ē | ēr | ī | ō | ŏŏ | ôr | ow | oy | ū | zh | ə |
|---|---|---|---|---|---|---|---|---|---|---|---|---|---|---|
| day | air | far | her | bee | tear | light | rope | book | for | cow | boy | tune | vision | item |

| Day 3 | | Day 4 | |
|---|---|---|---|
| 1. ____________________ | ☐ | 1. ____________________ | ☐ |
| 2. ____________________ | ☐ | 2. ____________________ | ☐ |
| 3. ____________________ | ☐ | 3. ____________________ | ☐ |
| 4. ____________________ | ☐ | 4. ____________________ | ☐ |
| 5. ____________________ | ☐ | 5. ____________________ | ☐ |
| 6. ____________________ | ☐ | 6. ____________________ | ☐ |
| 7. ____________________ | ☐ | 7. ____________________ | ☐ |
| 8. ____________________ | ☐ | 8. ____________________ | ☐ |
| 9. ____________________ | ☐ | 9. ____________________ | ☐ |
| 10. ____________________ | ☐ | 10. ____________________ | ☐ |
| 11. ____________________ | ☐ | 11. ____________________ | ☐ |
| 12. ____________________ | ☐ | 12. ____________________ | ☐ |
| 13. ____________________ | ☐ | 13. ____________________ | ☐ |
| 14. ____________________ | ☐ | 14. ____________________ | ☐ |
| 15. ____________________ | ☐ | 15. ____________________ | ☐ |
| 16. ____________________ | ☐ | 16. ____________________ | ☐ |
| 17. ____________________ | ☐ | 17. ____________________ | ☐ |
| 18. ____________________ | ☐ | 18. ____________________ | ☐ |
| 19. ____________________ | ☐ | 19. ____________________ | ☐ |
| 20. ____________________ | ☐ | 20. ____________________ | ☐ |

| ā | âr | är | er | ē | ēr | ī | ō | ŏŏ | ôr | ow | oy | ū | zh | ə |
|---|---|---|---|---|---|---|---|---|---|---|---|---|---|---|
| day | air | far | her | bee | tear | light | rope | book | for | cow | boy | tune | vision | item |

# Lesson 9b

| | | | |
|---|---|---|---|
| 1. | ne ther ləndz | Netherlands | Ne$^{2}$ ther$^{4}$ lands$^{5}$ |
| 2. | am ster dam | Amsterdam | Am$^{2}$ ster$^{4}$ dam$^{3}$ |
| 3. | jer mə nē | Germany | Ger$^{3}$ man$^{3}$ y$^{1}$ |
| 4. | ber lin | Berlin | Ber$^{3}$ lin$^{3}$ |
| 5. | ad ə kwət | adequate | ad$^{2}$ e$^{1}$ quate$^{5}$ |
| 6. | kors (way or direction) | course | course$^{6}$ |
| 7. | kors (rough) | coarse | coarse$^{6}$ |
| 8. | in krēs | increase | in$^{2}$ crease$^{6}$ |
| 9. | dē krēs | decrease | de$^{2}$ crease$^{6}$ |
| 10. | a nə ver ser ē | anniversary | an$^{2}$ niv$^{3}$ er$^{2}$ sar$^{3}$ y$^{1}$ |
| 11. | pī ə nēr | pioneer | pi$^{2}$ o$^{1}$ neer$^{4}$ |
| 12. | tīp | type | type$^{4}$ |
| 13. | tip i kl | typical | typ$^{3}$ i$^{1}$ cal$^{3}$ |
| 14. | pos ə bl | possible | pos$^{3}$ si$^{2}$ ble$^{3}$ |
| 15. | pos ə blē | possibly | pos$^{3}$ si$^{2}$ bly$^{3}$ |
| 16. | | | |
| 17. | | | |
| 18. | | | |
| 19. | | | |
| 20. | | | |

| ā | âr | är | er | ē | ēr | ī | ō | ŏŏ | ôr | ow | oy | ū | zh | ə |
|---|---|---|---|---|---|---|---|---|---|---|---|---|---|---|
| day | air | far | her | bee | tear | light | rope | book | for | cow | boy | tune | vision | item |

*Syllable Savvy Spelling Six*

| Day 1 | | Day 2 | |
|---|---|---|---|
| 1. ________ | ☐ | 1. ________ | ☐ |
| 2. ________ | ☐ | 2. ________ | ☐ |
| 3. ________ | ☐ | 3. ________ | ☐ |
| 4. ________ | ☐ | 4. ________ | ☐ |
| 5. ________ | ☐ | 5. ________ | ☐ |
| 6. ________ | ☐ | 6. ________ | ☐ |
| 7. ________ | ☐ | 7. ________ | ☐ |
| 8. ________ | ☐ | 8. ________ | ☐ |
| 9. ________ | ☐ | 9. ________ | ☐ |
| 10. ________ | ☐ | 10. ________ | ☐ |
| 11. ________ | ☐ | 11. ________ | ☐ |
| 12. ________ | ☐ | 12. ________ | ☐ |
| 13. ________ | ☐ | 13. ________ | ☐ |
| 14. ________ | ☐ | 14. ________ | ☐ |
| 15. ________ | ☐ | 15. ________ | ☐ |
| 16. ________ | ☐ | 16. ________ | ☐ |
| 17. ________ | ☐ | 17. ________ | ☐ |
| 18. ________ | ☐ | 18. ________ | ☐ |
| 19. ________ | ☐ | 19. ________ | ☐ |
| 20. ________ | ☐ | 20. ________ | ☐ |

| ā | âr | är | er | ē | ēr | ī | ō | ŏŏ | ôr | ow | oy | ū | zh | ə |
|---|---|---|---|---|---|---|---|---|---|---|---|---|---|---|
| day | air | far | her | bee | tear | light | rope | book | for | cow | boy | tune | vision | item |

# Lesson 10

| | | | | |
|---|---|---|---|---|
| 1. | pō lənd | Poland | Po[2] land[4] | |
| 2. | wôr so | Warsaw | War[3] saw[3] | |
| 3. | swit zer lnd | Switzerland | Swit[4] zer[3] land[4] | |
| 4. | bern | Bern | Bern[4] | |
| 5. | ser vənt | servant | ser[3] vant[4] | |
| 6. | lā der | later | la[2] ter[3] | L |
| 7. | hīt | height | height[6] | S |
| 8. | wāt | weight | weight[6] | S |
| 9. | eg sī tid | excited | ex[2] ci[2] ted[3] | J |
| 10. | lōn lē | lonely | lone[4] ly[2] | |
| 11. | sercht | searched | search[6]ed[2] | J |
| 12. | fôr ist | forest | for[3] est[3] | |
| 13. | shep erd | shepherd | shep[4] herd[4] | |
| 14. | o pə zit | opposite | op[2] po[2] site[4] | |
| 15. | o fəl | awful | aw[2] ful[3] | |
| 16. | | | | |
| 17. | | | | |
| 18. | | | | |
| 19. | | | | |
| 20. | | | | |

| ā | âr | är | er | ē | ēr | ī | ō | o͝o | ôr | ow | oy | ū | zh | ə |
|---|---|---|---|---|---|---|---|---|---|---|---|---|---|---|
| day | air | far | her | bee | tear | light | rope | book | for | cow | boy | tune | vision | item |

Day 3

1. ____________________ ☐
2. ____________________ ☐
3. ____________________ ☐
4. ____________________ ☐
5. ____________________ ☐
6. ____________________ ☐
7. ____________________ ☐
8. ____________________ ☐
9. ____________________ ☐
10. ____________________ ☐
11. ____________________ ☐
12. ____________________ ☐
13. ____________________ ☐
14. ____________________ ☐
15. ____________________ ☐
16. ____________________ ☐
17. ____________________ ☐
18. ____________________ ☐
19. ____________________ ☐
20. ____________________ ☐

Day 4

1. ____________________ ☐
2. ____________________ ☐
3. ____________________ ☐
4. ____________________ ☐
5. ____________________ ☐
6. ____________________ ☐
7. ____________________ ☐
8. ____________________ ☐
9. ____________________ ☐
10. ____________________ ☐
11. ____________________ ☐
12. ____________________ ☐
13. ____________________ ☐
14. ____________________ ☐
15. ____________________ ☐
16. ____________________ ☐
17. ____________________ ☐
18. ____________________ ☐
19. ____________________ ☐
20. ____________________ ☐



| ā | âr | är | er | ē | ēr | ī | ō | ŏŏ | ôr | ow | oy | ū | zh | ə |
|---|---|---|---|---|---|---|---|---|---|---|---|---|---|---|
| day | air | far | her | bee | tear | light | rope | book | for | cow | boy | tune | vision | item |

# Lesson 10b

| | | | |
|---|---|---|---|
| 1. | pō lənd | Poland | Po$^{2}$ land$^{4}$ |
| 2. | wôr so | Warsaw | War$^{3}$ saw$^{3}$ |
| 3. | swit zer lnd | Switzerland | Swit$^{4}$ zer$^{3}$ land$^{4}$ |
| 4. | bern | Bern | Bern$^{4}$ |
| 5. | ser vənt | servant | ser$^{3}$ vant$^{4}$ |
| 6. | lā der | later | la$^{2}$ ter$^{3}$ |
| 7. | hīt | height | height$^{6}$ |
| 8. | wāt | weight | weight$^{6}$ |
| 9. | eg sī tid | excited | ex$^{2}$ ci$^{2}$ ted$^{3}$ |
| 10. | lōn lē | lonely | lone$^{4}$ ly$^{2}$ |
| 11. | sercht | searched | search$^{6}$ed$^{2}$ |
| 12. | fôr ist | forest | for$^{3}$ est$^{3}$ |
| 13. | shep erd | shepherd | shep$^{4}$ herd$^{4}$ |
| 14. | o pə zit | opposite | op$^{2}$ po$^{2}$ site$^{4}$ |
| 15. | o fəl | awful | aw$^{2}$ ful$^{3}$ |
| 16. | | | |
| 17. | | | |
| 18. | | | |
| 19. | | | |
| 20. | | | |

| ā | âr | är | er | ē | ēr | ī | ō | ŏŏ | ôr | ow | oy | ū | zh | ə |
|---|---|---|---|---|---|---|---|---|---|---|---|---|---|---|
| day | air | far | her | bee | tear | light | rope | book | for | cow | boy | tune | vision | item |

*Syllable Savvy Spelling Six*

| Day 1 | | Day 2 | |
|---|---|---|---|
| 1. | ☐ | 1. | ☐ |
| 2. | ☐ | 2. | ☐ |
| 3. | ☐ | 3. | ☐ |
| 4. | ☐ | 4. | ☐ |
| 5. | ☐ | 5. | ☐ |
| 6. | ☐ | 6. | ☐ |
| 7. | ☐ | 7. | ☐ |
| 8. | ☐ | 8. | ☐ |
| 9. | ☐ | 9. | ☐ |
| 10. | ☐ | 10. | ☐ |
| 11. | ☐ | 11. | ☐ |
| 12. | ☐ | 12. | ☐ |
| 13. | ☐ | 13. | ☐ |
| 14. | ☐ | 14. | ☐ |
| 15. | ☐ | 15. | ☐ |
| 16. | ☐ | 16. | ☐ |
| 17. | ☐ | 17. | ☐ |
| 18. | ☐ | 18. | ☐ |
| 19. | ☐ | 19. | ☐ |
| 20. | ☐ | 20. | ☐ |

| **ā** | **âr** | **är** | **er** | **ē** | **ēr** | **ī** | **ō** | **ŏŏ** | **ôr** | **ow** | **oy** | **ū** | **zh** | **ə** |
|---|---|---|---|---|---|---|---|---|---|---|---|---|---|---|
| day | air | far | her | bee | tear | light | rope | book | for | cow | boy | tune | vision | item |

# Lesson 11

| | | | | |
|---|---|---|---|---|
| 1. | i də lē | Italy | I[1] ta[2] ly[2] | |
| 2. | rōm | Rome | Rome[4] | |
| 3. | grēs | Greece | Greece[6] | |
| 4. | a thins | Athens | A[1] thens[5] | |
| 5. | ad van tij | advantage | ad[2] van[3] tage[4] | |
| 6. | ə lert | alert | a[1] lert[4] | |
| 7. | voys | voice | voice[5] | |
| 8. | vō kl | vocal | vo[2] cal[3] | L |
| 9. | vol kā nō | volcano | vol[3] ca[2] no[2] | L |
| 10. | jer nē | journey | jour[4] ney[3] | |
| 11. | o səm | awesome | awe[3] some[4] | |
| 12. | mer sē | mercy | mer[3] cy[2] | |
| 13. | sko ler | scholar | scho[4] lar[3] | R |
| 14. | skə las tic | scholastic | scho[4] las[3] tic[3] | |
| 15. | pôr shn | portion | por[3] tion[4] | |
| 16. | | | | |
| 17. | | | | |
| 18. | | | | |
| 19. | | | | |
| 20. | | | | |

| ā | âr | är | er | ē | ēr | ī | ō | ŏŏ | ôr | ow | oy | ū | zh | ə |
|---|---|---|---|---|---|---|---|---|---|---|---|---|---|---|
| day | air | far | her | bee | tear | light | rope | book | for | cow | boy | tune | vision | item |

Syllable Savvy Spelling Six

| Day 3 | | Day 4 | |
|---|---|---|---|
| 1. | ☐ | 1. | ☐ |
| 2. | ☐ | 2. | ☐ |
| 3. | ☐ | 3. | ☐ |
| 4. | ☐ | 4. | ☐ |
| 5. | ☐ | 5. | ☐ |
| 6. | ☐ | 6. | ☐ |
| 7. | ☐ | 7. | ☐ |
| 8. | ☐ | 8. | ☐ |
| 9. | ☐ | 9. | ☐ |
| 10. | ☐ | 10. | ☐ |
| 11. | ☐ | 11. | ☐ |
| 12. | ☐ | 12. | ☐ |
| 13. | ☐ | 13. | ☐ |
| 14. | ☐ | 14. | ☐ |
| 15. | ☐ | 15. | ☐ |
| 16. | ☐ | 16. | ☐ |
| 17. | ☐ | 17. | ☐ |
| 18. | ☐ | 18. | ☐ |
| 19. | ☐ | 19. | ☐ |
| 20. | ☐ | 20. | ☐ |

| **ā** | **âr** | **är** | **er** | **ē** | **ēr** | **ī** | **ō** | **ŏŏ** | **ôr** | **ow** | **oy** | **ū** | **zh** | **ə** |
|---|---|---|---|---|---|---|---|---|---|---|---|---|---|---|
| day | air | far | her | bee | tear | light | rope | book | for | cow | boy | tune | vision | item |

# Lesson 11b

| | | | |
|---|---|---|---|
| 1. | i də lē | Italy | I[1] ta[2] ly[2] |
| 2. | rōm | Rome | Rome[4] |
| 3. | grēs | Greece | Greece[6] |
| 4. | a thins | Athens | A[1] thens[5] |
| 5. | ad van tij | advantage | ad[2] van[3] tage[4] |
| 6. | ə lert | alert | a[1] lert[4] |
| 7. | voys | voice | voice[5] |
| 8. | vō kl | vocal | vo[2] cal[3] |
| 9. | vol kā nō | volcano | vol[3] ca[2] no[2] |
| 10. | jer nē | journey | jour[4] ney[3] |
| 11. | o səm | awesome | awe[3] some[4] |
| 12. | mer sē | mercy | mer[3] cy[2] |
| 13. | sko ler | scholar | scho[4] lar[3] |
| 14. | skə las tic | scholastic | scho[4] las[3] tic[3] |
| 15. | pôr shn | portion | por[3] tion[4] |
| 16. | | | |
| 17. | | | |
| 18. | | | |
| 19. | | | |
| 20. | | | |

| ā | âr | är | er | ē | ēr | ī | ō | ŏŏ | ôr | ow | oy | ū | zh | ə |
|---|---|---|---|---|---|---|---|---|---|---|---|---|---|---|
| day | air | far | her | bee | tear | light | rope | book | for | cow | boy | tune | vision | item |

*Syllable Savvy Spelling Six*

| Day 1 | | Day 2 | |
|---|---|---|---|
| 1. | ☐ | 1. | ☐ |
| 2. | ☐ | 2. | ☐ |
| 3. | ☐ | 3. | ☐ |
| 4. | ☐ | 4. | ☐ |
| 5. | ☐ | 5. | ☐ |
| 6. | ☐ | 6. | ☐ |
| 7. | ☐ | 7. | ☐ |
| 8. | ☐ | 8. | ☐ |
| 9. | ☐ | 9. | ☐ |
| 10. | ☐ | 10. | ☐ |
| 11. | ☐ | 11. | ☐ |
| 12. | ☐ | 12. | ☐ |
| 13. | ☐ | 13. | ☐ |
| 14. | ☐ | 14. | ☐ |
| 15. | ☐ | 15. | ☐ |
| 16. | ☐ | 16. | ☐ |
| 17. | ☐ | 17. | ☐ |
| 18. | ☐ | 18. | ☐ |
| 19. | ☐ | 19. | ☐ |
| 20. | ☐ | 20. | ☐ |

| ā | âr | är | er | ē | ēr | ī | ō | ŏŏ | ôr | ow | oy | ū | zh | ə |
|---|---|---|---|---|---|---|---|---|---|---|---|---|---|---|
| day | air | far | her | bee | tear | light | rope | book | for | cow | boy | tune | vision | item |

# Lesson 12

| | | | | |
|---|---|---|---|---|
| 1. | al bān ē ə | Albania | Al$^2$ ban$^3$ i$^1$ a$^1$ | |
| 2. | ter o nə | Tirana | Tir$^3$ a$^1$ na$^2$ | |
| 3. | ä str ē ə | Austria | Au$^2$ stri$^4$ a$^1$ | |
| 4. | vē en ə | Vienna | Vi$^2$ en$^2$ na$^2$ | |
| 5. | in ter est ēn* | interesting | in$^2$ ter$^3$ es$^2$ ting$^4$ | G |
| 6. | pak əj | package | pack$^4$ age$^3$ | |
| 7. | ad vans | advance | ad$^2$ vance$^5$ | |
| 8. | ē ger | eager | ea$^2$ ger$^3$ | |
| 9. | pri vət lē | privately | pri$^3$ vate$^4$ ly$^2$ | |
| 10. | skwer əl | squirrel | squir$^5$ rel$^3$ | |
| 11. | trī umf | triumph | tri$^3$ umph$^4$ | |
| 12. | trī um fənt | triumphant | tri$^3$ um$^2$ phant$^5$ | |
| 13. | do ter | daughter | daugh$^5$ ter$^3$ | P |
| 14. | fôr chən | fortune | for$^3$ tune$^4$ | |
| 15. | fôr chə nət | fortunate | for$^3$ tun$^3$ ate$^3$ | |
| 16. | | | | |
| 17. | | | | |
| 18. | | | | |
| 19. | | | | |
| 20. | | | | |

| ā | âr | är | er | ē | ēr | ī | ō | ŏŏ | ôr | ow | oy | ū | zh | ə |
|---|---|---|---|---|---|---|---|---|---|---|---|---|---|---|
| day | air | far | her | bee | tear | light | rope | book | for | cow | boy | tune | vision | item |

| Day 3 | | Day 4 | |
|---|---|---|---|
| 1. | ☐ | 1. | ☐ |
| 2. | ☐ | 2. | ☐ |
| 3. | ☐ | 3. | ☐ |
| 4. | ☐ | 4. | ☐ |
| 5. | ☐ | 5. | ☐ |
| 6. | ☐ | 6. | ☐ |
| 7. | ☐ | 7. | ☐ |
| 8. | ☐ | 8. | ☐ |
| 9. | ☐ | 9. | ☐ |
| 10. | ☐ | 10. | ☐ |
| 11. | ☐ | 11. | ☐ |
| 12. | ☐ | 12. | ☐ |
| 13. | ☐ | 13. | ☐ |
| 14. | ☐ | 14. | ☐ |
| 15. | ☐ | 15. | ☐ |
| 16. | ☐ | 16. | ☐ |
| 17. | ☐ | 17. | ☐ |
| 18. | ☐ | 18. | ☐ |
| 19. | ☐ | 19. | ☐ |
| 20. | ☐ | 20. | ☐ |

| **ā** | **âr** | **är** | **er** | **ē** | **ēr** | **ī** | **ō** | **ŏŏ** | **ôr** | **ow** | **oy** | **ū** | **zh** | **ə** |
|---|---|---|---|---|---|---|---|---|---|---|---|---|---|---|
| day | air | far | her | bee | tear | light | rope | book | for | cow | boy | tune | vision | item |

# Lesson 12b

| | | | |
|---|---|---|---|
| 1. | al bān ē ə | Albania | Al$^2$ ban$^3$ i$^1$ a$^1$ |
| 2. | ter o nə | Tirana | Tir$^3$ a$^1$ na$^2$ |
| 3. | ä str ē ə | Austria | Au$^2$ stri$^4$ a$^1$ |
| 4. | vē en ə | Vienna | Vi$^2$ en$^2$ na$^2$ |
| 5. | in ter est ēn* | interesting | in$^2$ ter$^3$ es$^2$ ting$^4$ |
| 6. | pak əj | package | pack$^4$ age$^3$ |
| 7. | ad vans | advance | ad$^2$ vance$^5$ |
| 8. | ē ger | eager | ea$^2$ ger$^3$ |
| 9. | pri vət lē | privately | pri$^3$ vate$^4$ ly$^2$ |
| 10. | skwer əl | squirrel | squir$^5$ rel$^3$ |
| 11. | trī umf | triumph | tri$^3$ umph$^4$ |
| 12. | trī um fənt | triumphant | tri$^3$ um$^2$ phant$^5$ |
| 13. | do ter | daughter | daugh$^5$ ter$^3$ |
| 14. | fôr chən | fortune | for$^3$ tune$^4$ |
| 15. | fôr chə nət | fortunate | for$^3$ tun$^3$ ate$^3$ |
| 16. | | | |
| 17. | | | |
| 18. | | | |
| 19. | | | |
| 20. | | | |

| ā | âr | är | er | ē | ēr | ī | ō | ŏŏ | ôr | ow | oy | ū | zh | ə |
|---|---|---|---|---|---|---|---|---|---|---|---|---|---|---|
| day | air | far | her | bee | tear | light | rope | book | for | cow | boy | tune | vision | item |

Syllable Savvy Spelling Six

## Day 1

1. ______________________ ☐
2. ______________________ ☐
3. ______________________ ☐
4. ______________________ ☐
5. ______________________ ☐
6. ______________________ ☐
7. ______________________ ☐
8. ______________________ ☐
9. ______________________ ☐
10. ______________________ ☐
11. ______________________ ☐
12. ______________________ ☐
13. ______________________ ☐
14. ______________________ ☐
15. ______________________ ☐
16. ______________________ ☐
17. ______________________ ☐
18. ______________________ ☐
19. ______________________ ☐
20. ______________________ ☐

## Day 2

1. ______________________ ☐
2. ______________________ ☐
3. ______________________ ☐
4. ______________________ ☐
5. ______________________ ☐
6. ______________________ ☐
7. ______________________ ☐
8. ______________________ ☐
9. ______________________ ☐
10. ______________________ ☐
11. ______________________ ☐
12. ______________________ ☐
13. ______________________ ☐
14. ______________________ ☐
15. ______________________ ☐
16. ______________________ ☐
17. ______________________ ☐
18. ______________________ ☐
19. ______________________ ☐
20. ______________________ ☐

| ā | âr | är | er | ē | ēr | ī | ō | ŏŏ | ôr | ow | oy | ū | zh | ə |
|---|---|---|---|---|---|---|---|---|---|---|---|---|---|---|
| day | air | far | her | bee | tear | light | rope | book | for | cow | boy | tune | vision | item |

# Lesson 13

| | | | | |
|---|---|---|---|---|
| 1. | hun ger ē | Hungary | Hun$^3$ gar$^3$ y$^1$ | |
| 2. | bū də pest | Budapest | Bu$^2$ da$^2$ pest$^4$ | |
| 3. | bos nē ə | Bosnia | Bos$^3$ ni$^2$ a$^1$ | |
| 4. | sâr ā yā vō | Sarajevo | Sar$^3$ a$^1$ je$^2$ vo$^2$ | |
| 5. | kam er ə* | camera | ca$^2$ me$^2$ ra$^2$ | G |
| 6. | drôr | drawer | draw$^4$er$^2$ | |
| 7. | er lē er | earlier | ear$^3$ li$^2$ er$^2$ | C |
| 8. | re gyū ler | regular | re$^2$ gu$^2$ lar$^3$ | |
| 9. | rē lā tid | related | re$^2$ la$^2$ ted$^3$ | |
| 10. | eks er sīz | exercise | ex$^2$ er$^2$ cise$^4$ | |
| 11. | thēf | thief | thief$^5$ | S |
| 12. | thēvz | thieves | thieves$^7$ | E |
| 13. | i ni shəl | initial | i$^1$ ni$^2$ tial$^4$ | T |
| 14. | prī mâr ē | primary | pri$^3$ mar$^3$ y$^1$ | |
| 15. | se kən dâr ē | secondary | se$^2$ con$^3$ dar$^3$ y$^1$ | |
| 16. | | | | |
| 17. | | | | |
| 18. | | | | |
| 19. | | | | |
| 20. | | | | |

| ā | âr | är | er | ē | ēr | ī | ō | ŏŏ | ôr | ow | oy | ū | zh | ə |
|---|---|---|---|---|---|---|---|---|---|---|---|---|---|---|
| day | air | far | her | bee | tear | light | rope | book | for | cow | boy | tune | vision | item |

*Syllable Savvy Spelling Six*

| Day 3 | | Day 4 | |
|---|---|---|---|
| 1. | ☐ | 1. | ☐ |
| 2. | ☐ | 2. | ☐ |
| 3. | ☐ | 3. | ☐ |
| 4. | ☐ | 4. | ☐ |
| 5. | ☐ | 5. | ☐ |
| 6. | ☐ | 6. | ☐ |
| 7. | ☐ | 7. | ☐ |
| 8. | ☐ | 8. | ☐ |
| 9. | ☐ | 9. | ☐ |
| 10. | ☐ | 10. | ☐ |
| 11. | ☐ | 11. | ☐ |
| 12. | ☐ | 12. | ☐ |
| 13. | ☐ | 13. | ☐ |
| 14. | ☐ | 14. | ☐ |
| 15. | ☐ | 15. | ☐ |
| 16. | ☐ | 16. | ☐ |
| 17. | ☐ | 17. | ☐ |
| 18. | ☐ | 18. | ☐ |
| 19. | ☐ | 19. | ☐ |
| 20. | ☐ | 20. | ☐ |

| ā | âr | är | er | ē | ēr | ī | ō | ŏŏ | ôr | ow | oy | ū | zh | ə |
|---|---|---|---|---|---|---|---|---|---|---|---|---|---|---|
| day | air | far | her | bee | tear | light | rope | book | for | cow | boy | tune | vision | item |

# Lesson 13b

| | | | |
|---|---|---|---|
| 1. | hun ger ē | Hungary | Hun[3] gar[3] y[1] |
| 2. | bū də pest | Budapest | Bu[2] da[2] pest[4] |
| 3. | bos nē ə | Bosnia | Bos[3] ni[2] a[1] |
| 4. | sâr ā yā vō | Sarajevo | Sar[3] a[1] je[2] vo[2] |
| 5. | kam er ə* | camera | ca[2] me[2] ra[2] |
| 6. | drôr | drawer | draw[4]er[2] |
| 7. | er lē er | earlier | ear[3] li[2] er[2] |
| 8. | re gyū ler | regular | re[2] gu[2] lar[3] |
| 9. | rē lā tid | related | re[2] la[2] ted[3] |
| 10. | eks er sīz | exercise | ex[2] er[2] cise[4] |
| 11. | thēf | thief | thief[5] |
| 12. | thēvz | thieves | thieves[7] |
| 13. | i ni shəl | initial | i[1] ni[2] tial[4] |
| 14. | prī mâr ē | primary | pri[3] mar[3] y[1] |
| 15. | se kən dâr ē | secondary | se[2] con[3] dar[3] y[1] |
| 16. | | | |
| 17. | | | |
| 18. | | | |
| 19. | | | |
| 20. | | | |

| ā | âr | är | er | ē | ēr | ī | ō | ŏŏ | ôr | ow | oy | ū | zh | ə |
|---|---|---|---|---|---|---|---|---|---|---|---|---|---|---|
| day | air | far | her | bee | tear | light | rope | book | for | cow | boy | tune | vision | item |

| Day 1 | | Day 2 | |
|---|---|---|---|
| 1. | ☐ | 1. | ☐ |
| 2. | ☐ | 2. | ☐ |
| 3. | ☐ | 3. | ☐ |
| 4. | ☐ | 4. | ☐ |
| 5. | ☐ | 5. | ☐ |
| 6. | ☐ | 6. | ☐ |
| 7. | ☐ | 7. | ☐ |
| 8. | ☐ | 8. | ☐ |
| 9. | ☐ | 9. | ☐ |
| 10. | ☐ | 10. | ☐ |
| 11. | ☐ | 11. | ☐ |
| 12. | ☐ | 12. | ☐ |
| 13. | ☐ | 13. | ☐ |
| 14. | ☐ | 14. | ☐ |
| 15. | ☐ | 15. | ☐ |
| 16. | ☐ | 16. | ☐ |
| 17. | ☐ | 17. | ☐ |
| 18. | ☐ | 18. | ☐ |
| 19. | ☐ | 19. | ☐ |
| 20. | ☐ | 20. | ☐ |

| **ā** | **âr** | **är** | **er** | **ē** | **ēr** | **ī** | **ō** | **o͝o** | **ôr** | **ow** | **oy** | **ū** | **zh** | **ə** |
|---|---|---|---|---|---|---|---|---|---|---|---|---|---|---|
| day | air | far | her | bee | tear | light | rope | book | for | cow | boy | tune | vision | item |

# Lesson 14

| | | | | |
|---|---|---|---|---|
| 1. | ru shə | Russia | Rus$^{3}$ sia$^{3}$ | |
| 2. | mos kow | Moscow | Mos$^{3}$ cow$^{3}$ | |
| 3. | in dē ə | India | In$^{2}$ di$^{2}$ a$^{1}$ | |
| 4. | nū del hē | New Delhi | New$^{3}$ Del$^{3}$ hi$^{2}$ | |
| 5. | ə sīnd | assigned | as$^{2}$ sign$^{4}$ed$^{2}$ | J |
| 6. | prē ven tid | prevented | pre$^{3}$ vent$^{4}$ ed$^{2}$ | |
| 7. | kā pə bl | capable | ca$^{2}$ pa$^{2}$ ble$^{3}$ | L |
| 8. | rē lēf | relief | re$^{2}$ lief$^{4}$ | S |
| 9. | width | width | width$^{5}$ | |
| 10. | lē der ship | leadership | lea$^{3}$ der$^{3}$ ship$^{4}$ | |
| 11. | kown səl (group) | council | coun$^{4}$ cil$^{3}$ | |
| 12. | kown səl (advice) | counsel | coun$^{4}$ sel$^{3}$ | |
| 13. | rē dūsd | reduced | re$^{2}$ duc$^{3}$ed$^{2}$ | J |
| 14. | kōchd | coached | coach$^{5}$ed$^{2}$ | |
| 15. | ko pē rīt | copyright | co$^{2}$ py$^{2}$ right$^{5}$ | N |
| 16. | | | | |
| 17. | | | | |
| 18. | | | | |
| 19. | | | | |
| 20. | | | | |

| ā | âr | är | er | ē | ēr | ī | ō | ŏŏ | ôr | ow | oy | ū | zh | ə |
|---|---|---|---|---|---|---|---|---|---|---|---|---|---|---|
| day | air | far | her | bee | tear | light | rope | book | for | cow | boy | tune | vision | item |

*Syllable Savvy Spelling Six*

## Day 3

1. ________________ ☐
2. ________________ ☐
3. ________________ ☐
4. ________________ ☐
5. ________________ ☐
6. ________________ ☐
7. ________________ ☐
8. ________________ ☐
9. ________________ ☐
10. ________________ ☐
11. ________________ ☐
12. ________________ ☐
13. ________________ ☐
14. ________________ ☐
15. ________________ ☐
16. ________________ ☐
17. ________________ ☐
18. ________________ ☐
19. ________________ ☐
20. ________________ ☐

## Day 4

1. ________________ ☐
2. ________________ ☐
3. ________________ ☐
4. ________________ ☐
5. ________________ ☐
6. ________________ ☐
7. ________________ ☐
8. ________________ ☐
9. ________________ ☐
10. ________________ ☐
11. ________________ ☐
12. ________________ ☐
13. ________________ ☐
14. ________________ ☐
15. ________________ ☐
16. ________________ ☐
17. ________________ ☐
18. ________________ ☐
19. ________________ ☐
20. ________________ ☐

| ā | âr | är | er | ē | ēr | ī | ō | ŏŏ | ôr | ow | oy | ū | zh | ə |
|---|---|---|---|---|---|---|---|---|---|---|---|---|---|---|
| day | air | far | her | bee | tear | light | rope | book | for | cow | boy | tune | vision | item |

# Lesson 14b

| | | | |
|---|---|---|---|
| 1. | ru shə | Russia | Rus$^3$ sia$^3$ |
| 2. | mos kow | Moscow | Mos$^3$ cow$^3$ |
| 3. | in dē ə | India | In$^2$ di$^2$ a$^1$ |
| 4. | nū del hē | New Delhi | New$^3$ Del$^3$ hi$^2$ |
| 5. | ə sīnd | assigned | as$^2$ sign$^4$ed$^2$ |
| 6. | prē ven tid | prevented | pre$^3$ vent$^4$ ed$^2$ |
| 7. | kā pə bl | capable | ca$^2$ pa$^2$ ble$^3$ |
| 8. | rē lēf | relief | re$^2$ lief$^4$ |
| 9. | width | width | width$^5$ |
| 10. | lē der ship | leadership | lea$^3$ der$^3$ ship$^4$ |
| 11. | kown səl (group) | council | coun$^4$ cil$^3$ |
| 12. | kown səl (advice) | counsel | coun$^4$ sel$^3$ |
| 13. | rē dūsd | reduced | re$^2$ duc$^3$ed$^2$ |
| 14. | kōchd | coached | coach$^5$ed$^2$ |
| 15. | ko pē rīt | copyright | co$^2$ py$^2$ right$^5$ |
| 16. | | | |
| 17. | | | |
| 18. | | | |
| 19. | | | |
| 20. | | | |

| ā | âr | är | er | ē | ēr | ī | ō | ŏŏ | ôr | ow | oy | ū | zh | ə |
|---|---|---|---|---|---|---|---|---|---|---|---|---|---|---|
| day | air | far | her | bee | tear | light | rope | book | for | cow | boy | tune | vision | item |

*Syllable Savvy Spelling Six*

## Day 1

1. ________ ☐
2. ________ ☐
3. ________ ☐
4. ________ ☐
5. ________ ☐
6. ________ ☐
7. ________ ☐
8. ________ ☐
9. ________ ☐
10. ________ ☐
11. ________ ☐
12. ________ ☐
13. ________ ☐
14. ________ ☐
15. ________ ☐
16. ________ ☐
17. ________ ☐
18. ________ ☐
19. ________ ☐
20. ________ ☐

## Day 2

1. ________ ☐
2. ________ ☐
3. ________ ☐
4. ________ ☐
5. ________ ☐
6. ________ ☐
7. ________ ☐
8. ________ ☐
9. ________ ☐
10. ________ ☐
11. ________ ☐
12. ________ ☐
13. ________ ☐
14. ________ ☐
15. ________ ☐
16. ________ ☐
17. ________ ☐
18. ________ ☐
19. ________ ☐
20. ________ ☐

| **ā** | **âr** | **är** | **er** | **ē** | **ēr** | **ī** | **ō** | **ŏŏ** | **ôr** | **ow** | **oy** | **ū** | **zh** | **ə** |
|---|---|---|---|---|---|---|---|---|---|---|---|---|---|---|
| day | air | far | her | bee | tear | light | rope | book | for | cow | boy | tune | vision | item |

# Lesson 15

| | | | | |
|---|---|---|---|---|
| 1. | nə pol | Nepal | Ne$^{2}$ pal$^{3}$ | |
| 2. | koth mon dū | Kathmandu | Kath$^{4}$ man$^{3}$ du$^{2}$ | |
| 3. | bong lə desh | Bangladesh | Bang$^{4}$ la$^{2}$ desh$^{4}$ | |
| 4. | do kə | Dhaka | Dha$^{3}$ ka$^{2}$ | |
| 5. | ker əj | courage | cour$^{4}$ age$^{3}$ | |
| 6. | in ker əj | encourage | en$^{2}$ cour$^{4}$ age$^{3}$ | |
| 7. | priv ə lij* | privilege | priv$^{4}$ i$^{1}$ lege$^{4}$ | G |
| 8. | sə fīs | suffice | suf$^{3}$ fice$^{4}$ | |
| 9. | sə fi shint | sufficient | suf$^{3}$ fi$^{2}$ cient$^{5}$ | S |
| 10. | bē gun | begun | be$^{2}$ gun$^{3}$ | |
| 11. | we ther (sun or rain) | weather | wea$^{3}$ ther$^{4}$ | |
| 12. | we ther (if) | whether | whe$^{3}$ ther$^{4}$ | |
| 13. | bi zē | busy | bu$^{2}$ sy$^{2}$ | |
| 14. | biz ē nis | busyness | bu$^{2}$ sy$^{2}$ ness$^{4}$ | |
| 15. | biz ə nis* | business | bu$^{2}$ si$^{2}$ ness$^{4}$ | C |
| 16. | | | | |
| 17. | | | | |
| 18. | | | | |
| 19. | | | | |
| 20. | | | | |

| ā | âr | är | er | ē | ēr | ī | ō | ŏŏ | ôr | ow | oy | ū | zh | ə |
|---|---|---|---|---|---|---|---|---|---|---|---|---|---|---|
| day | air | far | her | bee | tear | light | rope | book | for | cow | boy | tune | vision | item |

## Day 3

1. ______ ☐
2. ______ ☐
3. ______ ☐
4. ______ ☐
5. ______ ☐
6. ______ ☐
7. ______ ☐
8. ______ ☐
9. ______ ☐
10. ______ ☐
11. ______ ☐
12. ______ ☐
13. ______ ☐
14. ______ ☐
15. ______ ☐
16. ______ ☐
17. ______ ☐
18. ______ ☐
19. ______ ☐
20. ______ ☐

## Day 4

1. ______ ☐
2. ______ ☐
3. ______ ☐
4. ______ ☐
5. ______ ☐
6. ______ ☐
7. ______ ☐
8. ______ ☐
9. ______ ☐
10. ______ ☐
11. ______ ☐
12. ______ ☐
13. ______ ☐
14. ______ ☐
15. ______ ☐
16. ______ ☐
17. ______ ☐
18. ______ ☐
19. ______ ☐
20. ______ ☐

| ā | âr | är | er | ē | ēr | ī | ō | ŏŏ | ôr | ow | oy | ū | zh | ə |
|---|---|---|---|---|---|---|---|---|---|---|---|---|---|---|
| day | air | far | her | bee | tear | light | rope | book | for | cow | boy | tune | vision | item |

# Lesson 15b

| | | | |
|---|---|---|---|
| 1. | nə pol | Nepal | Ne$^2$ pal$^3$ |
| 2. | koth mon dū | Kathmandu | Kath$^4$ man$^3$ du$^2$ |
| 3. | bong lə desh | Bangladesh | Bang$^4$ la$^2$ desh$^4$ |
| 4. | do kə | Dhaka | Dha$^3$ ka$^2$ |
| 5. | ker əj | courage | cour$^4$ age$^3$ |
| 6. | in ker əj | encourage | en$^2$ cour$^4$ age$^3$ |
| 7. | priv ə lij* | privilege | priv$^4$ i$^1$ lege$^4$ |
| 8. | sə fīs | suffice | suf$^3$ fice$^4$ |
| 9. | sə fi shint | sufficient | suf$^3$ fi$^2$ cient$^5$ |
| 10. | bē gun | begun | be$^2$ gun$^3$ |
| 11. | we ther (sun or rain) | weather | wea$^3$ ther$^4$ |
| 12. | we ther (if) | whether | whe$^3$ ther$^4$ |
| 13. | bi zē | busy | bu$^2$ sy$^2$ |
| 14. | biz ē nis | busyness | bu$^2$ sy$^2$ ness$^4$ |
| 15. | biz ə nis* | business | bu$^2$ si$^2$ ness$^4$ |
| 16. | | | |
| 17. | | | |
| 18. | | | |
| 19. | | | |
| 20. | | | |

| ā | âr | är | er | ē | ēr | ī | ō | ŏŏ | ôr | ow | oy | ū | zh | ə |
|---|---|---|---|---|---|---|---|---|---|---|---|---|---|---|
| day | air | far | her | bee | tear | light | rope | book | for | cow | boy | tune | vision | item |

*Syllable Savvy Spelling Six*

| Day 1 | | | Day 2 | | |
|---|---|---|---|---|---|
| 1. | ______________________ | ☐ | 1. | ______________________ | ☐ |
| 2. | ______________________ | ☐ | 2. | ______________________ | ☐ |
| 3. | ______________________ | ☐ | 3. | ______________________ | ☐ |
| 4. | ______________________ | ☐ | 4. | ______________________ | ☐ |
| 5. | ______________________ | ☐ | 5. | ______________________ | ☐ |
| 6. | ______________________ | ☐ | 6. | ______________________ | ☐ |
| 7. | ______________________ | ☐ | 7. | ______________________ | ☐ |
| 8. | ______________________ | ☐ | 8. | ______________________ | ☐ |
| 9. | ______________________ | ☐ | 9. | ______________________ | ☐ |
| 10. | ______________________ | ☐ | 10. | ______________________ | ☐ |
| 11. | ______________________ | ☐ | 11. | ______________________ | ☐ |
| 12. | ______________________ | ☐ | 12. | ______________________ | ☐ |
| 13. | ______________________ | ☐ | 13. | ______________________ | ☐ |
| 14. | ______________________ | ☐ | 14. | ______________________ | ☐ |
| 15. | ______________________ | ☐ | 15. | ______________________ | ☐ |
| 16. | ______________________ | ☐ | 16. | ______________________ | ☐ |
| 17. | ______________________ | ☐ | 17. | ______________________ | ☐ |
| 18. | ______________________ | ☐ | 18. | ______________________ | ☐ |
| 19. | ______________________ | ☐ | 19. | ______________________ | ☐ |
| 20. | ______________________ | ☐ | 20. | ______________________ | ☐ |

| ā | âr | är | er | ē | ēr | ī | ō | ŏŏ | ôr | ow | oy | ū | zh | ə |
|---|---|---|---|---|---|---|---|---|---|---|---|---|---|---|
| day | air | far | her | bee | tear | light | rope | book | for | cow | boy | tune | vision | item |

# Lesson 16

| | | | | |
|---|---|---|---|---|
| 1. | chī nə | China | Chi$^{3}$ na$^{2}$ | |
| 2. | bā zhing | Beijing | Bei$^{3}$ jing$^{4}$ | |
| 3. | kam bō dē ə | Cambodia | Cam$^{3}$ bo$^{2}$ di$^{2}$ a$^{1}$ | |
| 4. | nom pen | Phnom Penh | Phnom$^{5}$ Penh$^{4}$ | |
| 5. | ə tachd | attached | at$^{2}$ tach$^{4}$ed$^{2}$ | J |
| 6. | ō kā zhən | occasion | oc$^{2}$ ca$^{2}$ sion$^{4}$ | |
| 7. | re kə mend | recommend | re$^{2}$ com$^{3}$ mend$^{4}$ | |
| 8. | lūz (not win) | lose | lose$^{4}$ | |
| 9. | lūs (not stuck) | loose | loose$^{5}$ | |
| 10. | ə mung | among | a$^{1}$ mong$^{4}$ | |
| 11. | eks pēr ē ins | experience | ex$^{2}$ per$^{3}$ i$^{1}$ ence$^{4}$ | M |
| 12. | plez ənt | pleasant | pleas$^{5}$ ant$^{3}$ | |
| 13. | ath lēt | athlete | ath$^{3}$ lete$^{4}$ | |
| 14. | ath le dic | athletic | ath$^{3}$ le$^{2}$ tic$^{3}$ | |
| 15. | dis ə pēr | disappear | dis$^{3}$ ap$^{2}$ pear$^{4}$ | |
| 16. | | | | |
| 17. | | | | |
| 18. | | | | |
| 19. | | | | |
| 20. | | | | |

| ā | âr | är | er | ē | ēr | ī | ō | ŏŏ | ôr | ow | oy | ū | zh | ə |
|---|---|---|---|---|---|---|---|---|---|---|---|---|---|---|
| day | air | far | her | bee | tear | light | rope | book | for | cow | boy | tune | vision | item |

Syllable Savvy Spelling Six

Day 3

1. ______________________ ☐
2. ______________________ ☐
3. ______________________ ☐
4. ______________________ ☐
5. ______________________ ☐
6. ______________________ ☐
7. ______________________ ☐
8. ______________________ ☐
9. ______________________ ☐
10. ______________________ ☐
11. ______________________ ☐
12. ______________________ ☐
13. ______________________ ☐
14. ______________________ ☐
15. ______________________ ☐
16. ______________________ ☐
17. ______________________ ☐
18. ______________________ ☐
19. ______________________ ☐
20. ______________________ ☐

Day 4

1. ______________________ ☐
2. ______________________ ☐
3. ______________________ ☐
4. ______________________ ☐
5. ______________________ ☐
6. ______________________ ☐
7. ______________________ ☐
8. ______________________ ☐
9. ______________________ ☐
10. ______________________ ☐
11. ______________________ ☐
12. ______________________ ☐
13. ______________________ ☐
14. ______________________ ☐
15. ______________________ ☐
16. ______________________ ☐
17. ______________________ ☐
18. ______________________ ☐
19. ______________________ ☐
20. ______________________ ☐

| **ā** | **âr** | **är** | **er** | **ē** | **ēr** | **ī** | **ō** | **ŏŏ** | **ôr** | **ow** | **oy** | **ū** | **zh** | **ə** |
|---|---|---|---|---|---|---|---|---|---|---|---|---|---|---|
| day | air | far | her | bee | tear | light | rope | book | for | cow | boy | tune | vision | item |

# Lesson 16b

| | | | |
|---|---|---|---|
| 1. | chī nə | China | Chi$^{3}$ na$^{2}$ |
| 2. | bā zhing | Beijing | Bei$^{3}$ jing$^{4}$ |
| 3. | kam bō dē ə | Cambodia | Cam$^{3}$ bo$^{2}$ di$^{2}$ a$^{1}$ |
| 4. | nom pen | Phnom Penh | Phnom$^{5}$ Penh$^{4}$ |
| 5. | ə tachd | attached | at$^{2}$ tach$^{4}$ed$^{2}$ |
| 6. | ō kā zhən | occasion | oc$^{2}$ ca$^{2}$ sion$^{4}$ |
| 7. | re kə mend | recommend | re$^{2}$ com$^{3}$ mend$^{4}$ |
| 8. | lūz (not win) | lose | lose$^{4}$ |
| 9. | lūs (not stuck) | loose | loose$^{5}$ |
| 10. | ə mung | among | a$^{1}$ mong$^{4}$ |
| 11. | eks pēr ē ins | experience | ex$^{2}$ per$^{3}$ i$^{1}$ ence$^{4}$ |
| 12. | plez ənt | pleasant | pleas$^{5}$ ant$^{3}$ |
| 13. | ath lēt | athlete | ath$^{3}$ lete$^{4}$ |
| 14. | ath le dic | athletic | ath$^{3}$ le$^{2}$ tic$^{3}$ |
| 15. | dis ə pēr | disappear | dis$^{3}$ ap$^{2}$ pear$^{4}$ |
| 16. | | | |
| 17. | | | |
| 18. | | | |
| 19. | | | |
| 20. | | | |

| ā | âr | är | er | ē | ēr | ī | ō | ŏŏ | ôr | ow | oy | ū | zh | ə |
|---|---|---|---|---|---|---|---|---|---|---|---|---|---|---|
| day | air | far | her | bee | tear | light | rope | book | for | cow | boy | tune | vision | item |

*Syllable Savvy Spelling Six*

Day 1

1. ______________________ ☐
2. ______________________ ☐
3. ______________________ ☐
4. ______________________ ☐
5. ______________________ ☐
6. ______________________ ☐
7. ______________________ ☐
8. ______________________ ☐
9. ______________________ ☐
10. ______________________ ☐
11. ______________________ ☐
12. ______________________ ☐
13. ______________________ ☐
14. ______________________ ☐
15. ______________________ ☐
16. ______________________ ☐
17. ______________________ ☐
18. ______________________ ☐
19. ______________________ ☐
20. ______________________ ☐

Day 2

1. ______________________ ☐
2. ______________________ ☐
3. ______________________ ☐
4. ______________________ ☐
5. ______________________ ☐
6. ______________________ ☐
7. ______________________ ☐
8. ______________________ ☐
9. ______________________ ☐
10. ______________________ ☐
11. ______________________ ☐
12. ______________________ ☐
13. ______________________ ☐
14. ______________________ ☐
15. ______________________ ☐
16. ______________________ ☐
17. ______________________ ☐
18. ______________________ ☐
19. ______________________ ☐
20. ______________________ ☐

| **ā** | **âr** | **är** | **er** | **ē** | **ēr** | **ī** | **ō** | **ŏŏ** | **ôr** | **ow** | **oy** | **ū** | **zh** | **ə** |
|---|---|---|---|---|---|---|---|---|---|---|---|---|---|---|
| day | air | far | her | bee | tear | light | rope | book | for | cow | boy | tune | vision | item |

# Lesson 17

| | | | |
|---|---|---|---|
| 1. | kôr ē ə | Korea | Kor$^{3}$ e$^{1}$ a$^{1}$ |
| 2. | sē ōl | Seoul | Se$^{2}$ oul$^{3}$ |
| 3. | jə pan | Japan | Ja$^{2}$ pan$^{3}$ |
| 4. | tō kē o | Tokyo | To$^{2}$ ky$^{2}$ o$^{1}$ |
| 5. | min ət | minute | min$^{3}$ ute$^{3}$ |
| 6. | fôr dē | forty | for$^{3}$ ty$^{2}$ |
| 7. | per fôrm | perform | per$^{3}$ form$^{4}$ |
| 8. | per fôrm əns | performance | per$^{3}$ for$^{3}$ mance$^{5}$ |
| 9. | stīl | style | style$^{5}$ |
| 10. | dŏŏr ēn | during | dur$^{3}$ ing$^{3}$ |
| 11. | ek səl ənt | excellent | ex$^{2}$ cel$^{3}$ lent$^{4}$ |
| 12. | ek səl əns | excellence | ex$^{2}$ cel$^{3}$ lence$^{5}$ |
| 13. | yôr (belongs to you) | your | your$^{4}$ |
| 14. | yôr (you are) | you're | you$^{3}$ 're$^{3}$ |
| 15. | sə pōz | suppose | sup$^{3}$ pose$^{4}$ |
| 16. | | | |
| 17. | | | |
| 18. | | | |
| 19. | | | |
| 20. | | | |

U

L

| ā | âr | är | er | ē | ēr | ī | ō | ŏŏ | ôr | ow | oy | ū | zh | ə |
|---|---|---|---|---|---|---|---|---|---|---|---|---|---|---|
| day | air | far | her | bee | tear | light | rope | book | for | cow | boy | tune | vision | item |

Day 3

1. ______________________ ☐
2. ______________________ ☐
3. ______________________ ☐
4. ______________________ ☐
5. ______________________ ☐
6. ______________________ ☐
7. ______________________ ☐
8. ______________________ ☐
9. ______________________ ☐
10. ______________________ ☐
11. ______________________ ☐
12. ______________________ ☐
13. ______________________ ☐
14. ______________________ ☐
15. ______________________ ☐
16. ______________________ ☐
17. ______________________ ☐
18. ______________________ ☐
19. ______________________ ☐
20. ______________________ ☐

Day 4

1. ______________________ ☐
2. ______________________ ☐
3. ______________________ ☐
4. ______________________ ☐
5. ______________________ ☐
6. ______________________ ☐
7. ______________________ ☐
8. ______________________ ☐
9. ______________________ ☐
10. ______________________ ☐
11. ______________________ ☐
12. ______________________ ☐
13. ______________________ ☐
14. ______________________ ☐
15. ______________________ ☐
16. ______________________ ☐
17. ______________________ ☐
18. ______________________ ☐
19. ______________________ ☐
20. ______________________ ☐

| ā | âr | är | er | ē | ēr | ī | ō | ŏŏ | ôr | ow | oy | ū | zh | ə |
|---|---|---|---|---|---|---|---|---|---|---|---|---|---|---|
| day | air | far | her | bee | tear | light | rope | book | for | cow | boy | tune | vision | item |

# Lesson 17b

| | | | |
|---|---|---|---|
| 1. | kôr ē ə | Korea | Kor$^3$ e$^1$ a$^1$ |
| 2. | sē ōl | Seoul | Se$^2$ oul$^3$ |
| 3. | jə pan | Japan | Ja$^2$ pan$^3$ |
| 4. | tō kē o | Tokyo | To$^2$ ky$^2$ o$^1$ |
| 5. | min ət | minute | min$^3$ ute$^3$ |
| 6. | fôr dē | forty | for$^3$ ty$^2$ |
| 7. | per fôrm | perform | per$^3$ form$^4$ |
| 8. | per fôrm əns | performance | per$^3$ for$^3$ mance$^5$ |
| 9. | stīl | style | style$^5$ |
| 10. | dŏŏr ēn | during | dur$^3$ ing$^3$ |
| 11. | ek səl ənt | excellent | ex$^2$ cel$^3$ lent$^4$ |
| 12. | ek səl əns | excellence | ex$^2$ cel$^3$ lence$^5$ |
| 13. | yôr (belongs to you) | your | your$^4$ |
| 14. | yôr (you are) | you're | you$^3$ 're$^3$ |
| 15. | sə pōz | suppose | sup$^3$ pose$^4$ |
| 16. | | | |
| 17. | | | |
| 18. | | | |
| 19. | | | |
| 20. | | | |

| ā | âr | är | er | ē | ēr | ī | ō | ŏŏ | ôr | ow | oy | ū | zh | ə |
|---|---|---|---|---|---|---|---|---|---|---|---|---|---|---|
| day | air | far | her | bee | tear | light | rope | book | for | cow | boy | tune | vision | item |

*Syllable Savvy Spelling Six*

| Day 1 | | Day 2 | |
|---|---|---|---|
| 1. ______ | ☐ | 1. ______ | ☐ |
| 2. ______ | ☐ | 2. ______ | ☐ |
| 3. ______ | ☐ | 3. ______ | ☐ |
| 4. ______ | ☐ | 4. ______ | ☐ |
| 5. ______ | ☐ | 5. ______ | ☐ |
| 6. ______ | ☐ | 6. ______ | ☐ |
| 7. ______ | ☐ | 7. ______ | ☐ |
| 8. ______ | ☐ | 8. ______ | ☐ |
| 9. ______ | ☐ | 9. ______ | ☐ |
| 10. ______ | ☐ | 10. ______ | ☐ |
| 11. ______ | ☐ | 11. ______ | ☐ |
| 12. ______ | ☐ | 12. ______ | ☐ |
| 13. ______ | ☐ | 13. ______ | ☐ |
| 14. ______ | ☐ | 14. ______ | ☐ |
| 15. ______ | ☐ | 15. ______ | ☐ |
| 16. ______ | ☐ | 16. ______ | ☐ |
| 17. ______ | ☐ | 17. ______ | ☐ |
| 18. ______ | ☐ | 18. ______ | ☐ |
| 19. ______ | ☐ | 19. ______ | ☐ |
| 20. ______ | ☐ | 20. ______ | ☐ |

| **ā** | **âr** | **är** | **er** | **ē** | **ēr** | **ī** | **ō** | **o͝o** | **ôr** | **ow** | **oy** | **ū** | **zh** | **ə** |
|---|---|---|---|---|---|---|---|---|---|---|---|---|---|---|
| day | air | far | her | bee | tear | light | rope | book | for | cow | boy | tune | vision | item |

# Lesson 18

| | | | |
|---|---|---|---|
| 1. | tī land | Thailand | Thai$^{4}$ land$^{4}$ |
| 2. | bang kok | Bangkok | Bang$^{4}$ kok$^{3}$ |
| 4. | fil ə pēnz | Philippines | Phil$^{4}$ ip$^{2}$ pines$^{5}$ |
| 5. | mə nil ə | Manila | Ma$^{2}$ ni$^{2}$ la$^{2}$ |
| 5. | rē mem berd | remembered | re$^{2}$ mem$^{3}$ ber$^{3}$ed$^{2}$ |
| 6. | lī brâr rē | library | li$^{2}$ brar$^{4}$ y$^{1}$ |
| 7. | tā ler | tailor | tai$^{3}$ lor$^{3}$ |
| 8. | nēs | niece | niece$^{5}$ |
| 9. | nef yū | nephew | neph$^{4}$ ew$^{2}$ |
| 10. | chōz | chose | chose$^{5}$ |
| 11. | chō zən | chosen | cho$^{3}$ sen$^{3}$ |
| 12. | nīn dē | ninety | nine$^{4}$ ty$^{2}$ |
| 13. | ə genst | against | a$^{1}$ gainst$^{6}$ |
| 14. | ē kwip | equip | e$^{1}$ quip$^{4}$ |
| 15. | ē kwip mint | equipment | e$^{1}$ quip$^{4}$ ment$^{4}$ |
| 16. | | | |
| 17. | | | |
| 18. | | | |
| 19. | | | |
| 20. | | | |

J

Q

S

| ā | âr | är | er | ē | ēr | ī | ō | ŏŏ | ôr | ow | oy | ū | zh | ə |
|---|---|---|---|---|---|---|---|---|---|---|---|---|---|---|
| day | air | far | her | bee | tear | light | rope | book | for | cow | boy | tune | vision | item |

*Syllable Savvy Spelling Six*

## Day 3

1. ________________ ☐
2. ________________ ☐
3. ________________ ☐
4. ________________ ☐
5. ________________ ☐
6. ________________ ☐
7. ________________ ☐
8. ________________ ☐
9. ________________ ☐
10. ________________ ☐
11. ________________ ☐
12. ________________ ☐
13. ________________ ☐
14. ________________ ☐
15. ________________ ☐
16. ________________ ☐
17. ________________ ☐
18. ________________ ☐
19. ________________ ☐
20. ________________ ☐

## Day 4

1. ________________ ☐
2. ________________ ☐
3. ________________ ☐
4. ________________ ☐
5. ________________ ☐
6. ________________ ☐
7. ________________ ☐
8. ________________ ☐
9. ________________ ☐
10. ________________ ☐
11. ________________ ☐
12. ________________ ☐
13. ________________ ☐
14. ________________ ☐
15. ________________ ☐
16. ________________ ☐
17. ________________ ☐
18. ________________ ☐
19. ________________ ☐
20. ________________ ☐

| ā | âr | är | er | ē | ēr | ī | ō | ŏŏ | ôr | ow | oy | ū | zh | ə |
|---|---|---|---|---|---|---|---|---|---|---|---|---|---|---|
| day | air | far | her | bee | tear | light | rope | book | for | cow | boy | tune | vision | item |

# Lesson 18b

| | | | |
|---|---|---|---|
| 1. | tī land | Thailand | Thai$^4$ land$^4$ |
| 2. | bang kok | Bangkok | Bang$^4$ kok$^3$ |
| 4. | fil ə pēnz | Philippines | Phil$^4$ ip$^2$ pines$^5$ |
| 5. | mə nil ə | Manila | Ma$^2$ ni$^2$ la$^2$ |
| 5. | rē mem berd | remembered | re$^2$ mem$^3$ ber$^3$ed$^2$ |
| 6. | lī brâr rē | library | li$^2$ brar$^4$ y$^1$ |
| 7. | tā ler | tailor | tai$^3$ lor$^3$ |
| 8. | nēs | niece | niece$^5$ |
| 9. | nef yū | nephew | neph$^4$ ew$^2$ |
| 10. | chōz | chose | chose$^5$ |
| 11. | chō zən | chosen | cho$^3$ sen$^3$ |
| 12. | nīn dē | ninety | nine$^4$ ty$^2$ |
| 13. | ə genst | against | a$^1$ gainst$^6$ |
| 14. | ē kwip | equip | e$^1$ quip$^4$ |
| 15. | ē kwip mint | equipment | e$^1$ quip$^4$ ment$^4$ |
| 16. | | | |
| 17. | | | |
| 18. | | | |
| 19. | | | |
| 20. | | | |

| ā | âr | är | er | ē | ēr | ī | ō | ŏŏ | ôr | ow | oy | ū | zh | ə |
|---|---|---|---|---|---|---|---|---|---|---|---|---|---|---|
| day | air | far | her | bee | tear | light | rope | book | for | cow | boy | tune | vision | item |

Syllable Savvy Spelling Six

| Day 1 | | Day 2 | |
|---|---|---|---|
| 1. ________ | ☐ | 1. ________ | ☐ |
| 2. ________ | ☐ | 2. ________ | ☐ |
| 3. ________ | ☐ | 3. ________ | ☐ |
| 4. ________ | ☐ | 4. ________ | ☐ |
| 5. ________ | ☐ | 5. ________ | ☐ |
| 6. ________ | ☐ | 6. ________ | ☐ |
| 7. ________ | ☐ | 7. ________ | ☐ |
| 8. ________ | ☐ | 8. ________ | ☐ |
| 9. ________ | ☐ | 9. ________ | ☐ |
| 10. ________ | ☐ | 10. ________ | ☐ |
| 11. ________ | ☐ | 11. ________ | ☐ |
| 12. ________ | ☐ | 12. ________ | ☐ |
| 13. ________ | ☐ | 13. ________ | ☐ |
| 14. ________ | ☐ | 14. ________ | ☐ |
| 15. ________ | ☐ | 15. ________ | ☐ |
| 16. ________ | ☐ | 16. ________ | ☐ |
| 17. ________ | ☐ | 17. ________ | ☐ |
| 18. ________ | ☐ | 18. ________ | ☐ |
| 19. ________ | ☐ | 19. ________ | ☐ |
| 20. ________ | ☐ | 20. ________ | ☐ |

| **ā** | **âr** | **är** | **er** | **ē** | **ēr** | **ī** | **ō** | **ŏŏ** | **ôr** | **ow** | **oy** | **ū** | **zh** | **ə** |
|---|---|---|---|---|---|---|---|---|---|---|---|---|---|---|
| day | air | far | her | bee | tear | light | rope | book | for | cow | boy | tune | vision | item |

# Lesson 19

| | | | | |
|---|---|---|---|---|
| 1. | o strāl yē ə | Australia | Au$^2$ stral$^5$ i$^1$ a$^1$ | |
| 2. | kan ber ə | Canberra | Can$^3$ ber$^3$ ra$^2$ | |
| 3. | nū zē lənd | New Zealand | New$^3$ Zea$^3$ land$^4$ | |
| 4. | wel ēn tən | Wellington | Wel$^3$ ling$^4$ ton$^3$ | |
| 5. | dān jer | danger | dan$^3$ ger$^3$ | |
| 6. | kâr rē ēn | carrying | car$^3$ ry$^2$ ing$^3$ | |
| 7. | kâr ē əj* | carriage | car$^3$ riage$^5$ | C |
| 8. | prâr ē | prairie | prair$^5$ ie$^2$ | |
| 9. | flōr əl | floral | flor$^4$ al$^2$ | |
| 10. | chär mēn | charming | charm$^5$ ing$^3$ | |
| 11. | dif i kəlt | difficult | dif$^3$ fi$^2$ cult$^4$ | |
| 12. | dif i kəlt ēz | difficulties | dif$^3$ fi$^2$ cul$^3$ ties$^4$ | C |
| 13. | tēr fəl | tearful | tear$^4$ ful$^3$ | |
| 14. | tôr ment | torment | tor$^3$ ment$^4$ | |
| 15. | trū lē | truly | tru$^3$ ly$^2$ | L |
| 16. | | | | |
| 17. | | | | |
| 18. | | | | |
| 19. | | | | |
| 20. | | | | |

| ā | âr | är | er | ē | ēr | ī | ō | ŏŏ | ôr | ow | oy | ū | zh | ə |
|---|---|---|---|---|---|---|---|---|---|---|---|---|---|---|
| day | air | far | her | bee | tear | light | rope | book | for | cow | boy | tune | vision | item |

| Day 3 | | Day 4 | |
|---|---|---|---|
| 1. ____ | ☐ | 1. ____ | ☐ |
| 2. ____ | ☐ | 2. ____ | ☐ |
| 3. ____ | ☐ | 3. ____ | ☐ |
| 4. ____ | ☐ | 4. ____ | ☐ |
| 5. ____ | ☐ | 5. ____ | ☐ |
| 6. ____ | ☐ | 6. ____ | ☐ |
| 7. ____ | ☐ | 7. ____ | ☐ |
| 8. ____ | ☐ | 8. ____ | ☐ |
| 9. ____ | ☐ | 9. ____ | ☐ |
| 10. ____ | ☐ | 10. ____ | ☐ |
| 11. ____ | ☐ | 11. ____ | ☐ |
| 12. ____ | ☐ | 12. ____ | ☐ |
| 13. ____ | ☐ | 13. ____ | ☐ |
| 14. ____ | ☐ | 14. ____ | ☐ |
| 15. ____ | ☐ | 15. ____ | ☐ |
| 16. ____ | ☐ | 16. ____ | ☐ |
| 17. ____ | ☐ | 17. ____ | ☐ |
| 18. ____ | ☐ | 18. ____ | ☐ |
| 19. ____ | ☐ | 19. ____ | ☐ |
| 20. ____ | ☐ | 20. ____ | ☐ |

| ā | âr | är | er | ē | ēr | ī | ō | ŏŏ | ôr | ow | oy | ū | zh | ə |
|---|---|---|---|---|---|---|---|---|---|---|---|---|---|---|
| day | air | far | her | bee | tear | light | rope | book | for | cow | boy | tune | vision | item |

# Lesson 19b

| | | | |
|---|---|---|---|
| 1. | o strāl yē ə | Australia | Au$^{2}$ stral$^{5}$ i$^{1}$ a$^{1}$ |
| 2. | kan ber ə | Canberra | Can$^{3}$ ber$^{3}$ ra$^{2}$ |
| 3. | nū zē lənd | New Zealand | New$^{3}$ Zea$^{3}$ land$^{4}$ |
| 4. | wel ēn tən | Wellington | Wel$^{3}$ ling$^{4}$ ton$^{3}$ |
| 5. | dān jer | danger | dan$^{3}$ ger$^{3}$ |
| 6. | kâr rē ēn | carrying | car$^{3}$ ry$^{2}$ ing$^{3}$ |
| 7. | kâr ē əj* | carriage | car$^{3}$ riage$^{5}$ |
| 8. | prâr ē | prairie | prair$^{5}$ ie$^{2}$ |
| 9. | flōr əl | floral | flor$^{4}$ al$^{2}$ |
| 10. | chär mēn | charming | charm$^{5}$ ing$^{3}$ |
| 11. | dif i kəlt | difficult | dif$^{3}$ fi$^{2}$ cult$^{4}$ |
| 12. | dif i kəlt ēz | difficulties | dif$^{3}$ fi$^{2}$ cul$^{3}$ ties$^{4}$ |
| 13. | tēr fəl | tearful | tear$^{4}$ ful$^{3}$ |
| 14. | tôr ment | torment | tor$^{3}$ ment$^{4}$ |
| 15. | trū lē | truly | tru$^{3}$ ly$^{2}$ |
| 16. | | | |
| 17. | | | |
| 18. | | | |
| 19. | | | |
| 20. | | | |

| ā | âr | är | er | ē | ēr | ī | ō | ŏŏ | ôr | ow | oy | ū | zh | ə |
|---|---|---|---|---|---|---|---|---|---|---|---|---|---|---|
| day | air | far | her | bee | tear | light | rope | book | for | cow | boy | tune | vision | item |

*Syllable Savvy Spelling Six*

| Day 1 | | Day 2 | |
|---|---|---|---|
| **1.** | ☐ | **1.** | ☐ |
| **2.** | ☐ | **2.** | ☐ |
| **3.** | ☐ | **3.** | ☐ |
| **4.** | ☐ | **4.** | ☐ |
| **5.** | ☐ | **5.** | ☐ |
| **6.** | ☐ | **6.** | ☐ |
| **7.** | ☐ | **7.** | ☐ |
| **8.** | ☐ | **8.** | ☐ |
| **9.** | ☐ | **9.** | ☐ |
| **10.** | ☐ | **10.** | ☐ |
| **11.** | ☐ | **11.** | ☐ |
| **12.** | ☐ | **12.** | ☐ |
| **13.** | ☐ | **13.** | ☐ |
| **14.** | ☐ | **14.** | ☐ |
| **15.** | ☐ | **15.** | ☐ |
| **16.** | ☐ | **16.** | ☐ |
| **17.** | ☐ | **17.** | ☐ |
| **18.** | ☐ | **18.** | ☐ |
| **19.** | ☐ | **19.** | ☐ |
| **20.** | ☐ | **20.** | ☐ |

| **ā** | **âr** | **är** | **er** | **ē** | **ēr** | **ī** | **ō** | **ŏŏ** | **ôr** | **ow** | **oy** | **ū** | **zh** | **ə** |
|---|---|---|---|---|---|---|---|---|---|---|---|---|---|---|
| day | air | far | her | bee | tear | light | rope | book | for | cow | boy | tune | vision | item |

# Lesson 20

| | | | | |
|---|---|---|---|---|
| 1. | al jēr ē ə | Algeria | Al$^{2}$ ger$^{3}$ i$^{1}$ a$^{1}$ | M |
| 2. | al jērz | Algiers | Al$^{2}$ giers$^{5}$ | |
| 3. | lib ē ə | Libya | Lib$^{3}$ y$^{1}$ a$^{1}$ | |
| 4. | tri pō lē | Tripoli | Tri$^{3}$ po$^{2}$ li$^{2}$ | M |
| 5. | dan gl | dangle | dan$^{3}$ gle$^{3}$ | |
| 6. | choy siz | choices | choi$^{4}$ ces$^{3}$ | |
| 7. | tūerd | toured | tour$^{4}$ed$^{2}$ | J |
| 8. | ter i fik | terrific | ter$^{3}$ ri$^{2}$ fic$^{3}$ | |
| 9. | bə da zl | bedazzle | be$^{2}$ daz$^{3}$ zle$^{3}$ | |
| 10. | ə māz mint | amazement | a$^{1}$ maze$^{4}$ ment$^{4}$ | |
| 11. | plas ter | plaster | plas$^{4}$ ter$^{3}$ | |
| 12. | grow chē | grouchy | grou$^{4}$ chy$^{3}$ | |
| 13. | stri kn | stricken | strick$^{6}$ en$^{2}$ | |
| 14. | skūpd | scooped | scoop$^{5}$ed$^{2}$ | J |
| 15. | tri gerd | triggered | trig$^{4}$ ger$^{3}$ed$^{2}$ | J |
| 16. | | | | |
| 17. | | | | |
| 18. | | | | |
| 19. | | | | |
| 20. | | | | |

| ā | âr | är | er | ē | ēr | ī | ō | ŏŏ | ôr | ow | oy | ū | zh | ə |
|---|---|---|---|---|---|---|---|---|---|---|---|---|---|---|
| day | air | far | her | bee | tear | light | rope | book | for | cow | boy | tune | vision | item |

## Day 3

1. ______________________ ☐
2. ______________________ ☐
3. ______________________ ☐
4. ______________________ ☐
5. ______________________ ☐
6. ______________________ ☐
7. ______________________ ☐
8. ______________________ ☐
9. ______________________ ☐
10. ______________________ ☐
11. ______________________ ☐
12. ______________________ ☐
13. ______________________ ☐
14. ______________________ ☐
15. ______________________ ☐
16. ______________________ ☐
17. ______________________ ☐
18. ______________________ ☐
19. ______________________ ☐
20. ______________________ ☐

## Day 4

1. ______________________ ☐
2. ______________________ ☐
3. ______________________ ☐
4. ______________________ ☐
5. ______________________ ☐
6. ______________________ ☐
7. ______________________ ☐
8. ______________________ ☐
9. ______________________ ☐
10. ______________________ ☐
11. ______________________ ☐
12. ______________________ ☐
13. ______________________ ☐
14. ______________________ ☐
15. ______________________ ☐
16. ______________________ ☐
17. ______________________ ☐
18. ______________________ ☐
19. ______________________ ☐
20. ______________________ ☐

| **ā** | **âr** | **är** | **er** | **ē** | **ēr** | **ī** | **ō** | **ŏŏ** | **ôr** | **ow** | **oy** | **ū** | **zh** | **ə** |
|---|---|---|---|---|---|---|---|---|---|---|---|---|---|---|
| day | air | far | her | bee | tear | light | rope | book | for | cow | boy | tune | vision | item |

# Lesson 20b

| | | | |
|---|---|---|---|
| 1. | al jēr ē ə | Algeria | Al$^{2}$ ger$^{3}$ i$^{1}$ a$^{1}$ |
| 2. | al jērz | Algiers | Al$^{2}$ giers$^{5}$ |
| 3. | lib ē ə | Libya | Lib$^{3}$ y$^{1}$ a$^{1}$ |
| 4. | tri pō lē | Tripoli | Tri$^{3}$ po$^{2}$ li$^{2}$ |
| 5. | dan gl | dangle | dan$^{3}$ gle$^{3}$ |
| 6. | choy siz | choices | choi$^{4}$ ces$^{3}$ |
| 7. | tūerd | toured | tour$^{4}$ed$^{2}$ |
| 8. | ter i fik | terrific | ter$^{3}$ ri$^{2}$ fic$^{3}$ |
| 9. | bə da zl | bedazzle | be$^{2}$ daz$^{3}$ zle$^{3}$ |
| 10. | ə māz mint | amazement | a$^{1}$ maze$^{4}$ ment$^{4}$ |
| 11. | plas ter | plaster | plas$^{4}$ ter$^{3}$ |
| 12. | grow chē | grouchy | grou$^{4}$ chy$^{3}$ |
| 13. | stri kn | stricken | strick$^{6}$ en$^{2}$ |
| 14. | skūpd | scooped | scoop$^{5}$ed$^{2}$ |
| 15. | tri gerd | triggered | trig$^{4}$ ger$^{3}$ed$^{2}$ |
| 16. | | | |
| 17. | | | |
| 18. | | | |
| 19. | | | |
| 20. | | | |

| ā | âr | är | er | ē | ēr | ī | ō | ŏŏ | ôr | ow | oy | ū | zh | ə |
|---|---|---|---|---|---|---|---|---|---|---|---|---|---|---|
| day | air | far | her | bee | tear | light | rope | book | for | cow | boy | tune | vision | item |

*Syllable Savvy Spelling Six*

| Day 1 | | Day 2 | |
|---|---|---|---|
| 1. ______ | ☐ | 1. ______ | ☐ |
| 2. ______ | ☐ | 2. ______ | ☐ |
| 3. ______ | ☐ | 3. ______ | ☐ |
| 4. ______ | ☐ | 4. ______ | ☐ |
| 5. ______ | ☐ | 5. ______ | ☐ |
| 6. ______ | ☐ | 6. ______ | ☐ |
| 7. ______ | ☐ | 7. ______ | ☐ |
| 8. ______ | ☐ | 8. ______ | ☐ |
| 9. ______ | ☐ | 9. ______ | ☐ |
| 10. ______ | ☐ | 10. ______ | ☐ |
| 11. ______ | ☐ | 11. ______ | ☐ |
| 12. ______ | ☐ | 12. ______ | ☐ |
| 13. ______ | ☐ | 13. ______ | ☐ |
| 14. ______ | ☐ | 14. ______ | ☐ |
| 15. ______ | ☐ | 15. ______ | ☐ |
| 16. ______ | ☐ | 16. ______ | ☐ |
| 17. ______ | ☐ | 17. ______ | ☐ |
| 18. ______ | ☐ | 18. ______ | ☐ |
| 19. ______ | ☐ | 19. ______ | ☐ |
| 20. ______ | ☐ | 20. ______ | ☐ |

| **ā** | **âr** | **är** | **er** | **ē** | **ēr** | **ī** | **ō** | **ŏŏ** | **ôr** | **ow** | **oy** | **ū** | **zh** | **ə** |
|---|---|---|---|---|---|---|---|---|---|---|---|---|---|---|
| day | air | far | her | bee | tear | light | rope | book | for | cow | boy | tune | vision | item |

# Lesson 21

| | | | | |
|---|---|---|---|---|
| 1. | ē jipt | Egypt | E$^1$ gypt$^4$ | |
| 2. | kī rō | Cairo | Cai$^3$ ro$^2$ | |
| 3. | nī jer | Niger | Ni$^2$ ger$^3$ | |
| 4. | nī a mē | Niamey | Ni$^2$ a$^1$ mey$^3$ | |
| 5. | skôr pē ən | scorpion | scor$^4$ pi$^2$ on$^2$ | |
| 6. | re dē | ready | read$^4$ y$^1$ | |
| 7. | tem per ə men tl* | temperamental | tem$^3$ per$^3$ a$^1$ men$^3$ tal$^3$ | G |
| 8. | ə rānj | arrange | ar$^2$ range$^5$ | |
| 9. | spoy əl | spoil | spo$^3$ il$^2$ | |
| 10. | mēr er | mirror | mir$^3$ ror$^3$ | Q |
| 11. | shim er ēn | shimmering | shim$^4$ mer$^3$ ing$^3$ | K |
| 12. | in dekst | indexed | in$^2$ dex$^3$ed$^2$ | J |
| 13. | ə pin diks | appendix | ap$^2$ pen$^3$ dix$^3$ | |
| 14. | shär pin | sharpen | shar$^4$ pen$^3$ | |
| 15. | kā os | chaos | cha$^3$ os$^2$ | |
| 16. | | | | |
| 17. | | | | |
| 18. | | | | |
| 19. | | | | |
| 20. | | | | |

| ā | âr | är | er | ē | ēr | ī | ō | ŏŏ | ôr | ow | oy | ū | zh | ə |
|---|---|---|---|---|---|---|---|---|---|---|---|---|---|---|
| day | air | far | her | bee | tear | light | rope | book | for | cow | boy | tune | vision | item |

## Day 3

1. ____________________ ☐
2. ____________________ ☐
3. ____________________ ☐
4. ____________________ ☐
5. ____________________ ☐
6. ____________________ ☐
7. ____________________ ☐
8. ____________________ ☐
9. ____________________ ☐
10. ____________________ ☐
11. ____________________ ☐
12. ____________________ ☐
13. ____________________ ☐
14. ____________________ ☐
15. ____________________ ☐
16. ____________________ ☐
17. ____________________ ☐
18. ____________________ ☐
19. ____________________ ☐
20. ____________________ ☐

## Day 4

1. ____________________ ☐
2. ____________________ ☐
3. ____________________ ☐
4. ____________________ ☐
5. ____________________ ☐
6. ____________________ ☐
7. ____________________ ☐
8. ____________________ ☐
9. ____________________ ☐
10. ____________________ ☐
11. ____________________ ☐
12. ____________________ ☐
13. ____________________ ☐
14. ____________________ ☐
15. ____________________ ☐
16. ____________________ ☐
17. ____________________ ☐
18. ____________________ ☐
19. ____________________ ☐
20. ____________________ ☐

| **ā** | **âr** | **är** | **er** | **ē** | **ēr** | **ī** | **ō** | **ŏŏ** | **ôr** | **ow** | **oy** | **ū** | **zh** | **ə** |
|---|---|---|---|---|---|---|---|---|---|---|---|---|---|---|
| day | air | far | her | bee | tear | light | rope | book | for | cow | boy | tune | vision | item |

# Lesson 21b

| | | | |
|---|---|---|---|
| 1. | ē jipt | Egypt | E$^{1}$ gypt$^{4}$ |
| 2. | kī rō | Cairo | Cai$^{3}$ ro$^{2}$ |
| 3. | nī jer | Niger | Ni$^{2}$ ger$^{3}$ |
| 4. | nī a mē | Niamey | Ni$^{2}$ a$^{1}$ mey$^{3}$ |
| 5. | skôr pē ən | scorpion | scor$^{4}$ pi$^{2}$ on$^{2}$ |
| 6. | re dē | ready | read$^{4}$ y$^{1}$ |
| 7. | tem per ə men tl* | temperamental | tem$^{3}$ per$^{3}$ a$^{1}$ men$^{3}$ tal$^{3}$ |
| 8. | ə rānj | arrange | ar$^{2}$ range$^{5}$ |
| 9. | spoy əl | spoil | spo$^{3}$ il$^{2}$ |
| 10. | mēr er | mirror | mir$^{3}$ ror$^{3}$ |
| 11. | shim er ēn | shimmering | shim$^{4}$ mer$^{3}$ ing$^{3}$ |
| 12. | in dekst | indexed | in$^{2}$ dex$^{3}$ed$^{2}$ |
| 13. | ə pin diks | appendix | ap$^{2}$ pen$^{3}$ dix$^{3}$ |
| 14. | shär pin | sharpen | shar$^{4}$ pen$^{3}$ |
| 15. | kā os | chaos | cha$^{3}$ os$^{2}$ |
| 16. | | | |
| 17. | | | |
| 18. | | | |
| 19. | | | |
| 20. | | | |

| ā | âr | är | er | ē | ēr | ī | ō | ŏŏ | ôr | ow | oy | ū | zh | ə |
|---|---|---|---|---|---|---|---|---|---|---|---|---|---|---|
| day | air | far | her | bee | tear | light | rope | book | for | cow | boy | tune | vision | item |

*Syllable Savvy Spelling Six*

| Day 1 | | Day 2 | |
|---|---|---|---|
| 1. ________ | ☐ | 1. ________ | ☐ |
| 2. ________ | ☐ | 2. ________ | ☐ |
| 3. ________ | ☐ | 3. ________ | ☐ |
| 4. ________ | ☐ | 4. ________ | ☐ |
| 5. ________ | ☐ | 5. ________ | ☐ |
| 6. ________ | ☐ | 6. ________ | ☐ |
| 7. ________ | ☐ | 7. ________ | ☐ |
| 8. ________ | ☐ | 8. ________ | ☐ |
| 9. ________ | ☐ | 9. ________ | ☐ |
| 10. ________ | ☐ | 10. ________ | ☐ |
| 11. ________ | ☐ | 11. ________ | ☐ |
| 12. ________ | ☐ | 12. ________ | ☐ |
| 13. ________ | ☐ | 13. ________ | ☐ |
| 14. ________ | ☐ | 14. ________ | ☐ |
| 15. ________ | ☐ | 15. ________ | ☐ |
| 16. ________ | ☐ | 16. ________ | ☐ |
| 17. ________ | ☐ | 17. ________ | ☐ |
| 18. ________ | ☐ | 18. ________ | ☐ |
| 19. ________ | ☐ | 19. ________ | ☐ |
| 20. ________ | ☐ | 20. ________ | ☐ |

| **ā** | **âr** | **är** | **er** | **ē** | **ēr** | **ī** | **ō** | **ŏŏ** | **ôr** | **ow** | **oy** | **ū** | **zh** | **ə** |
|---|---|---|---|---|---|---|---|---|---|---|---|---|---|---|
| day | air | far | her | bee | tear | light | rope | book | for | cow | boy | tune | vision | item |

# Lesson 22

| | | | | |
|---|---|---|---|---|
| 1. | mō zam bēk | Mozambique | Mo$^{2}$ zam$^{3}$ bique$^{5}$ | |
| 2. | mə pū tō | Maputo | Ma$^{2}$ pu$^{2}$ to$^{2}$ | |
| 3. | ken yə | Kenya | Ken$^{3}$ ya$^{2}$ | |
| 4. | nī ro bē | Nairobi | Nai$^{3}$ ro$^{2}$ bi$^{2}$ | |
| 5. | volt | vault | vault$^{5}$ | |
| 6. | folt | fault | fault$^{5}$ | |
| 7. | pu zld | puzzled | puz$^{3}$ zl$^{2}$ed$^{2}$ | L |
| 8. | swift lē | swiftly | swift$^{5}$ ly$^{2}$ | |
| 9. | fla derd | flattered | flat$^{4}$ ter$^{3}$ed$^{2}$ | J |
| 10. | ker lē | curly | cur$^{3}$ ly$^{2}$ | |
| 11. | dē nī | deny | de$^{2}$ ny$^{2}$ | L |
| 12. | rē spond | respond | re$^{2}$ spond$^{5}$ | L |
| 13. | rē spon si bl | responsible | re$^{2}$ spon$^{4}$ si$^{2}$ ble$^{3}$ | |
| 14. | rē spon siv | responsive | re$^{2}$ spon$^{4}$ sive$^{4}$ | |
| 15. | krā zē | crazy | cra$^{3}$ zy$^{2}$ | L |
| 16. | | | | |
| 17. | | | | |
| 18. | | | | |
| 19. | | | | |
| 20. | | | | |

| ā | âr | är | er | ē | ēr | ī | ō | ŏŏ | ôr | ow | oy | ū | zh | ə |
|---|---|---|---|---|---|---|---|---|---|---|---|---|---|---|
| day | air | far | her | bee | tear | light | rope | book | for | cow | boy | tune | vision | item |

## Day 3

1. ______________________ ☐
2. ______________________ ☐
3. ______________________ ☐
4. ______________________ ☐
5. ______________________ ☐
6. ______________________ ☐
7. ______________________ ☐
8. ______________________ ☐
9. ______________________ ☐
10. ______________________ ☐
11. ______________________ ☐
12. ______________________ ☐
13. ______________________ ☐
14. ______________________ ☐
15. ______________________ ☐
16. ______________________ ☐
17. ______________________ ☐
18. ______________________ ☐
19. ______________________ ☐
20. ______________________ ☐

## Day 4

1. ______________________ ☐
2. ______________________ ☐
3. ______________________ ☐
4. ______________________ ☐
5. ______________________ ☐
6. ______________________ ☐
7. ______________________ ☐
8. ______________________ ☐
9. ______________________ ☐
10. ______________________ ☐
11. ______________________ ☐
12. ______________________ ☐
13. ______________________ ☐
14. ______________________ ☐
15. ______________________ ☐
16. ______________________ ☐
17. ______________________ ☐
18. ______________________ ☐
19. ______________________ ☐
20. ______________________ ☐

| **ā** | **âr** | **är** | **er** | **ē** | **ēr** | **ī** | **ō** | **ŏŏ** | **ôr** | **ow** | **oy** | **ū** | **zh** | **ə** |
|---|---|---|---|---|---|---|---|---|---|---|---|---|---|---|
| day | air | far | her | bee | tear | light | rope | book | for | cow | boy | tune | vision | item |

# Lesson 22b

| | | | |
|---|---|---|---|
| 1. | mō zam bēk | Mozambique | Mo$^{2}$ zam$^{3}$ bique$^{5}$ |
| 2. | mə pū tō | Maputo | Ma$^{2}$ pu$^{2}$ to$^{2}$ |
| 3. | ken yə | Kenya | Ken$^{3}$ ya$^{2}$ |
| 4. | nī ro bē | Nairobi | Nai$^{3}$ ro$^{2}$ bi$^{2}$ |
| 5. | volt | vault | vault$^{5}$ |
| 6. | folt | fault | fault$^{5}$ |
| 7. | pu zld | puzzled | puz$^{3}$ zl$^{2}$ed$^{2}$ |
| 8. | swift lē | swiftly | swift$^{5}$ ly$^{2}$ |
| 9. | fla derd | flattered | flat$^{4}$ ter$^{3}$ed$^{2}$ |
| 10. | ker lē | curly | cur$^{3}$ ly$^{2}$ |
| 11. | dē nī | deny | de$^{2}$ ny$^{2}$ |
| 12. | rē spond | respond | re$^{2}$ spond$^{5}$ |
| 13. | rē spon si bl | responsible | re$^{2}$ spon$^{4}$ si$^{2}$ ble$^{3}$ |
| 14. | rē spon siv | responsive | re$^{2}$ spon$^{4}$ sive$^{4}$ |
| 15. | krā zē | crazy | cra$^{3}$ zy$^{2}$ |
| 16. | | | |
| 17. | | | |
| 18. | | | |
| 19. | | | |
| 20. | | | |

| ā | âr | är | er | ē | ēr | ī | ō | ŏŏ | ôr | ow | oy | ū | zh | ə |
|---|---|---|---|---|---|---|---|---|---|---|---|---|---|---|
| day | air | far | her | bee | tear | light | rope | book | for | cow | boy | tune | vision | item |

*Syllable Savvy Spelling Six*

## Day 1

1. ______ ☐
2. ______ ☐
3. ______ ☐
4. ______ ☐
5. ______ ☐
6. ______ ☐
7. ______ ☐
8. ______ ☐
9. ______ ☐
10. ______ ☐
11. ______ ☐
12. ______ ☐
13. ______ ☐
14. ______ ☐
15. ______ ☐
16. ______ ☐
17. ______ ☐
18. ______ ☐
19. ______ ☐
20. ______ ☐

## Day 2

1. ______ ☐
2. ______ ☐
3. ______ ☐
4. ______ ☐
5. ______ ☐
6. ______ ☐
7. ______ ☐
8. ______ ☐
9. ______ ☐
10. ______ ☐
11. ______ ☐
12. ______ ☐
13. ______ ☐
14. ______ ☐
15. ______ ☐
16. ______ ☐
17. ______ ☐
18. ______ ☐
19. ______ ☐
20. ______ ☐

| ā | âr | är | er | ē | ēr | ī | ō | ŏŏ | ôr | ow | oy | ū | zh | ə |
|---|---|---|---|---|---|---|---|---|---|---|---|---|---|---|
| day | air | far | her | bee | tear | light | rope | book | for | cow | boy | tune | vision | item |

# Lesson 23

| | | | | |
|---|---|---|---|---|
| 1. | kan ə də | Canada | Can$^{3}$ a$^{1}$ da$^{2}$ | |
| 2. | o də wə | Ottawa | Ot$^{2}$ ta$^{2}$ wa$^{2}$ | |
| 3. | ū nī tid stāts | United States | U$^{1}$ ni$^{2}$ ted$^{3}$ States$^{6}$ | |
| 4. | wosh ēn tən dē sē | Washington D.C. | Wash$^{4}$ ing$^{3}$ ton$^{3}$ | |
| 5. | propd | propped | prop$^{4}$ped$^{3}$ | K |
| 6. | bôr der līn | borderline | bor$^{3}$ der$^{3}$ line$^{4}$ | |
| 7. | min ē ə cher* | miniature | min$^{3}$ i$^{1}$ a$^{1}$ ture$^{4}$ | G |
| 8. | ē ster | Easter | Eas$^{3}$ ter$^{3}$ | |
| 9. | də grē | degree | de$^{2}$ gree$^{4}$ | |
| 10. | fāl yer | failure | fail$^{4}$ ure$^{3}$ | |
| 11. | ran dəm | random | ran$^{3}$ dom$^{3}$ | |
| 12. | eks trēm lē | extremely | ex$^{2}$ treme$^{5}$ ly$^{2}$ | |
| 13. | pow er fl | powerful | pow$^{3}$ er$^{2}$ ful$^{3}$ | |
| 14. | fō dō gra fik | photographic | pho$^{3}$ to$^{2}$ graph$^{5}$ ic$^{2}$ | |
| 15. | strān | strain | strain$^{6}$ | |
| 16. | | | | |
| 17. | | | | |
| 18. | | | | |
| 19. | | | | |
| 20. | | | | |

| ā | âr | är | er | ē | ēr | ī | ō | ŏŏ | ôr | ow | oy | ū | zh | ə |
|---|---|---|---|---|---|---|---|---|---|---|---|---|---|---|
| day | air | far | her | bee | tear | light | rope | book | for | cow | boy | tune | vision | item |

Syllable Savvy Spelling Six

| Day 3 | | Day 4 | |
|---|---|---|---|
| 1. | ☐ | 1. | ☐ |
| 2. | ☐ | 2. | ☐ |
| 3. | ☐ | 3. | ☐ |
| 4. | ☐ | 4. | ☐ |
| 5. | ☐ | 5. | ☐ |
| 6. | ☐ | 6. | ☐ |
| 7. | ☐ | 7. | ☐ |
| 8. | ☐ | 8. | ☐ |
| 9. | ☐ | 9. | ☐ |
| 10. | ☐ | 10. | ☐ |
| 11. | ☐ | 11. | ☐ |
| 12. | ☐ | 12. | ☐ |
| 13. | ☐ | 13. | ☐ |
| 14. | ☐ | 14. | ☐ |
| 15. | ☐ | 15. | ☐ |
| 16. | ☐ | 16. | ☐ |
| 17. | ☐ | 17. | ☐ |
| 18. | ☐ | 18. | ☐ |
| 19. | ☐ | 19. | ☐ |
| 20. | ☐ | 20. | ☐ |

| ā | âr | är | er | ē | ēr | ī | ō | ŏŏ | ôr | ow | oy | ū | zh | ə |
|---|---|---|---|---|---|---|---|---|---|---|---|---|---|---|
| day | air | far | her | bee | tear | light | rope | book | for | cow | boy | tune | vision | item |

# Lesson 23b

| | | | |
|---|---|---|---|
| 1. | kan ə də | Canada | Can$^3$ a$^1$ da$^2$ |
| 2. | o də wə | Ottawa | Ot$^2$ ta$^2$ wa$^2$ |
| 3. | ū nī tid stāts | United States | U$^1$ ni$^2$ ted$^3$ States$^6$ |
| 4. | wosh ēn tən dē sē | Washington D.C. | Wash$^4$ ing$^3$ ton$^3$ |
| 5. | propd | propped | prop$^4$ped$^3$ |
| 6. | bôr der līn | borderline | bor$^3$ der$^3$ line$^4$ |
| 7. | min ē ə cher* | miniature | min$^3$ i$^1$ a$^1$ ture$^4$ |
| 8. | ē ster | Easter | Eas$^3$ ter$^3$ |
| 9. | də grē | degree | de$^2$ gree$^4$ |
| 10. | fāl yer | failure | fail$^4$ ure$^3$ |
| 11. | ran dəm | random | ran$^3$ dom$^3$ |
| 12. | eks trēm lē | extremely | ex$^2$ treme$^5$ ly$^2$ |
| 13. | pow er fl | powerful | pow$^3$ er$^2$ ful$^3$ |
| 14. | fō dō gra fik | photographic | pho$^3$ to$^2$ graph$^5$ ic$^2$ |
| 15. | strān | strain | strain$^6$ |
| 16. | | | |
| 17. | | | |
| 18. | | | |
| 19. | | | |
| 20. | | | |

| ā | âr | är | er | ē | ēr | ī | ō | ŏŏ | ôr | ow | oy | ū | zh | ə |
|---|---|---|---|---|---|---|---|---|---|---|---|---|---|---|
| day | air | far | her | bee | tear | light | rope | book | for | cow | boy | tune | vision | item |

| Day 1 | | Day 2 | |
|---|---|---|---|
| 1. | ☐ | 1. | ☐ |
| 2. | ☐ | 2. | ☐ |
| 3. | ☐ | 3. | ☐ |
| 4. | ☐ | 4. | ☐ |
| 5. | ☐ | 5. | ☐ |
| 6. | ☐ | 6. | ☐ |
| 7. | ☐ | 7. | ☐ |
| 8. | ☐ | 8. | ☐ |
| 9. | ☐ | 9. | ☐ |
| 10. | ☐ | 10. | ☐ |
| 11. | ☐ | 11. | ☐ |
| 12. | ☐ | 12. | ☐ |
| 13. | ☐ | 13. | ☐ |
| 14. | ☐ | 14. | ☐ |
| 15. | ☐ | 15. | ☐ |
| 16. | ☐ | 16. | ☐ |
| 17. | ☐ | 17. | ☐ |
| 18. | ☐ | 18. | ☐ |
| 19. | ☐ | 19. | ☐ |
| 20. | ☐ | 20. | ☐ |

| **ā** | **âr** | **är** | **er** | **ē** | **ēr** | **ī** | **ō** | **ŏŏ** | **ôr** | **ow** | **oy** | **ū** | **zh** | **ə** |
|---|---|---|---|---|---|---|---|---|---|---|---|---|---|---|
| day | air | far | her | bee | tear | light | rope | book | for | cow | boy | tune | vision | item |

# Lesson 24

| | | | |
|---|---|---|---|
| 1. | mek si kō | Mexico | Mex$^{3}$ i$^{1}$ co$^{2}$ |
| | | The Capital is Mexico City | |
| 2. | hā tē | Haiti | Hai$^{3}$ ti$^{2}$ |
| 3. | pôrt o prins | Port-au-Prince | Port$^{4}$ au$^{2}$ Prince$^{6}$ |
| 4. | suk ses | success | suc$^{3}$ cess$^{4}$ |
| 5. | in tens | intense | in$^{2}$ tense$^{5}$ |
| 6. | mag nə fī | magnify | mag$^{3}$ ni$^{2}$ fy$^{2}$ |
| 7. | mag ni fə snt | magnificent | mag$^{3}$ ni$^{2}$ fi$^{2}$ cent$^{4}$ |
| 8. | bri jis | bridges | brid$^{4}$ ges$^{3}$ |
| 9. | sī lns | silence | si$^{2}$ lence$^{5}$ |
| 10. | de nəm | denim | den$^{3}$ im$^{2}$ |
| 11. | ə lowd | aloud | a$^{1}$ loud$^{4}$ |
| 12. | wālz (cries) | wails | wails$^{5}$ |
| 13. | wālz (ocean mammal) | whales | whales$^{6}$ |
| 14. | wālz (country) | Wales | Wales$^{5}$ |
| 15. | rē plās mint | replacement | re$^{2}$ place$^{5}$ ment$^{4}$ |
| 16. | | | |
| 17. | | | |
| 18. | | | |
| 19. | | | |
| 20. | | | |

L

L

| ā | âr | är | er | ē | ēr | ī | ō | ŏŏ | ôr | ow | oy | ū | zh | ə |
|---|---|---|---|---|---|---|---|---|---|---|---|---|---|---|
| day | air | far | her | bee | tear | light | rope | book | for | cow | boy | tune | vision | item |

## Day 3

1. ______ ☐
2. ______ ☐
3. ______ ☐
4. ______ ☐
5. ______ ☐
6. ______ ☐
7. ______ ☐
8. ______ ☐
9. ______ ☐
10. ______ ☐
11. ______ ☐
12. ______ ☐
13. ______ ☐
14. ______ ☐
15. ______ ☐
16. ______ ☐
17. ______ ☐
18. ______ ☐
19. ______ ☐
20. ______ ☐

## Day 4

1. ______ ☐
2. ______ ☐
3. ______ ☐
4. ______ ☐
5. ______ ☐
6. ______ ☐
7. ______ ☐
8. ______ ☐
9. ______ ☐
10. ______ ☐
11. ______ ☐
12. ______ ☐
13. ______ ☐
14. ______ ☐
15. ______ ☐
16. ______ ☐
17. ______ ☐
18. ______ ☐
19. ______ ☐
20. ______ ☐

| ā | âr | är | er | ē | ēr | ī | ō | ŏŏ | ôr | ow | oy | ū | zh | ə |
|---|---|---|---|---|---|---|---|---|---|---|---|---|---|---|
| day | air | far | her | bee | tear | light | rope | book | for | cow | boy | tune | vision | item |

# Lesson 24b

| | | | |
|---|---|---|---|
| 1. | mek si kō | Mexico | Mex$^{3}$ i$^{1}$ co$^{2}$ |
| 2. | hā tē | Haiti | Hai$^{3}$ ti$^{2}$ |
| 3. | pôrt o prins | Port-au-Prince | Port$^{4}$ au$^{2}$ Prince$^{6}$ |
| 4. | suk ses | success | suc$^{3}$ cess$^{4}$ |
| 5. | in tens | intense | in$^{2}$ tense$^{5}$ |
| 6. | mag nə fī | magnify | mag$^{3}$ ni$^{2}$ fy$^{2}$ |
| 7. | mag ni fə snt | magnificent | mag$^{3}$ ni$^{2}$ fi$^{2}$ cent$^{4}$ |
| 8. | bri jis | bridges | brid$^{4}$ ges$^{3}$ |
| 9. | sī lns | silence | si$^{2}$ lence$^{5}$ |
| 10. | de nəm | denim | den$^{3}$ im$^{2}$ |
| 11. | ə lowd | aloud | a$^{1}$ loud$^{4}$ |
| 12. | wālz (cries) | wails | wails$^{5}$ |
| 13. | wālz (ocean mammal) | whales | whales$^{6}$ |
| 14. | wālz (country) | Wales | Wales$^{5}$ |
| 15. | rē plās mint | replacement | re$^{2}$ place$^{5}$ ment$^{4}$ |
| 16. | | | |
| 17. | | | |
| 18. | | | |
| 19. | | | |
| 20. | | | |

| ā | âr | är | er | ē | ēr | ī | ō | ŏŏ | ôr | ow | oy | ū | zh | ə |
|---|---|---|---|---|---|---|---|---|---|---|---|---|---|---|
| day | air | far | her | bee | tear | light | rope | book | for | cow | boy | tune | vision | item |

## Day 1

1. ____________________ ☐
2. ____________________ ☐
3. ____________________ ☐
4. ____________________ ☐
5. ____________________ ☐
6. ____________________ ☐
7. ____________________ ☐
8. ____________________ ☐
9. ____________________ ☐
10. ____________________ ☐
11. ____________________ ☐
12. ____________________ ☐
13. ____________________ ☐
14. ____________________ ☐
15. ____________________ ☐
16. ____________________ ☐
17. ____________________ ☐
18. ____________________ ☐
19. ____________________ ☐
20. ____________________ ☐

## Day 2

1. ____________________ ☐
2. ____________________ ☐
3. ____________________ ☐
4. ____________________ ☐
5. ____________________ ☐
6. ____________________ ☐
7. ____________________ ☐
8. ____________________ ☐
9. ____________________ ☐
10. ____________________ ☐
11. ____________________ ☐
12. ____________________ ☐
13. ____________________ ☐
14. ____________________ ☐
15. ____________________ ☐
16. ____________________ ☐
17. ____________________ ☐
18. ____________________ ☐
19. ____________________ ☐
20. ____________________ ☐

| **ā** | **âr** | **är** | **er** | **ē** | **ēr** | **ī** | **ō** | **ŏŏ** | **ôr** | **ow** | **oy** | **ū** | **zh** | **ə** |
|---|---|---|---|---|---|---|---|---|---|---|---|---|---|---|
| day | air | far | her | bee | tear | light | rope | book | for | cow | boy | tune | vision | item |

# Lesson 25

| | | | | |
|---|---|---|---|---|
| 1. | bə lēz | Belize | Be$^2$ lize$^4$ | |
| 2. | bel mō pan | Belmopan | Bel$^3$ mo$^2$ pan$^3$ | |
| 3. | el sal və dôr | El Salvador | El$^2$ Sal$^3$ va$^2$ dor$^3$ | |
| 4. | san sal və dôr | San Salvador | San$^3$ Sal$^3$ va$^2$ dor$^3$ | |
| 5. | dron | drawn | drawn$^5$ | |
| 6. | fo slz | fossils | fos$^3$ sils$^4$ | |
| 7. | chē dēn | cheating | cheat$^5$ ing$^3$ | |
| 8. | fyū cher | future | fu$^2$ ture$^4$ | L |
| 9. | vi dē ō | video | vid$^3$ e$^1$ o$^1$ | |
| 10. | star dl | startle | star$^4$ tle$^3$ | |
| 11. | star tl ēn | startling | star$^4$ tl$^2$ ing$^3$ | |
| 12. | cha pl | chapel | chap$^4$ el$^2$ | |
| 13. | kon sert | concert | con$^3$ cert$^4$ | |
| 14. | pro per dē | property | prop$^4$ er$^2$ ty$^2$ | L |
| 15. | do mi nōz | dominoes<br>Sometimes written 'dominos' | dom$^3$ i$^1$ noes$^4$ | |
| 16. | | | | |
| 17. | | | | |
| 18. | | | | |
| 19. | | | | |
| 20. | | | | |

| ā | âr | är | er | ē | ēr | ī | ō | ŏŏ | ôr | ow | oy | ū | zh | ə |
|---|---|---|---|---|---|---|---|---|---|---|---|---|---|---|
| day | air | far | her | bee | tear | light | rope | book | for | cow | boy | tune | vision | item |

## Day 3

1. ______________________ ☐
2. ______________________ ☐
3. ______________________ ☐
4. ______________________ ☐
5. ______________________ ☐
6. ______________________ ☐
7. ______________________ ☐
8. ______________________ ☐
9. ______________________ ☐
10. ______________________ ☐
11. ______________________ ☐
12. ______________________ ☐
13. ______________________ ☐
14. ______________________ ☐
15. ______________________ ☐
16. ______________________ ☐
17. ______________________ ☐
18. ______________________ ☐
19. ______________________ ☐
20. ______________________ ☐

## Day 4

1. ______________________ ☐
2. ______________________ ☐
3. ______________________ ☐
4. ______________________ ☐
5. ______________________ ☐
6. ______________________ ☐
7. ______________________ ☐
8. ______________________ ☐
9. ______________________ ☐
10. ______________________ ☐
11. ______________________ ☐
12. ______________________ ☐
13. ______________________ ☐
14. ______________________ ☐
15. ______________________ ☐
16. ______________________ ☐
17. ______________________ ☐
18. ______________________ ☐
19. ______________________ ☐
20. ______________________ ☐

| ā | âr | är | er | ē | ēr | ī | ō | ŏŏ | ôr | ow | oy | ū | zh | ə |
|---|---|---|---|---|---|---|---|---|---|---|---|---|---|---|
| day | air | far | her | bee | tear | light | rope | book | for | cow | boy | tune | vision | item |

# Lesson 25b

| | | | |
|---|---|---|---|
| 1. | bə lēz | Belize | Be$^{2}$ lize$^{4}$ |
| 2. | bel mō pan | Belmopan | Bel$^{3}$ mo$^{2}$ pan$^{3}$ |
| 3. | el sal və dôr | El Salvador | El$^{2}$ Sal$^{3}$ va$^{2}$ dor$^{3}$ |
| 4. | san sal və dôr | San Salvador | San$^{3}$ Sal$^{3}$ va$^{2}$ dor$^{3}$ |
| 5. | dron | drawn | drawn$^{5}$ |
| 6. | fo slz | fossils | fos$^{3}$ sils$^{4}$ |
| 7. | chē dēn | cheating | cheat$^{5}$ ing$^{3}$ |
| 8. | fyū cher | future | fu$^{2}$ ture$^{4}$ |
| 9. | vi dē ō | video | vid$^{3}$ e$^{1}$ o$^{1}$ |
| 10. | star dl | startle | star$^{4}$ tle$^{3}$ |
| 11. | star tl ēn | startling | star$^{4}$ tl$^{2}$ ing$^{3}$ |
| 12. | cha pl | chapel | chap$^{4}$ el$^{2}$ |
| 13. | kon sert | concert | con$^{3}$ cert$^{4}$ |
| 14. | pro per dē | property | prop$^{4}$ er$^{2}$ ty$^{2}$ |
| 15. | do mi nōz | dominoes | dom$^{3}$ i$^{1}$ noes$^{4}$ |
| 16. | | | |
| 17. | | | |
| 18. | | | |
| 19. | | | |
| 20. | | | |

| ā | âr | är | er | ē | ēr | ī | ō | ŏŏ | ôr | ow | oy | ū | zh | ə |
|---|---|---|---|---|---|---|---|---|---|---|---|---|---|---|
| day | air | far | her | bee | tear | light | rope | book | for | cow | boy | tune | vision | item |

## Day 1

1. ______________________ ☐
2. ______________________ ☐
3. ______________________ ☐
4. ______________________ ☐
5. ______________________ ☐
6. ______________________ ☐
7. ______________________ ☐
8. ______________________ ☐
9. ______________________ ☐
10. ______________________ ☐
11. ______________________ ☐
12. ______________________ ☐
13. ______________________ ☐
14. ______________________ ☐
15. ______________________ ☐
16. ______________________ ☐
17. ______________________ ☐
18. ______________________ ☐
19. ______________________ ☐
20. ______________________ ☐

## Day 2

1. ______________________ ☐
2. ______________________ ☐
3. ______________________ ☐
4. ______________________ ☐
5. ______________________ ☐
6. ______________________ ☐
7. ______________________ ☐
8. ______________________ ☐
9. ______________________ ☐
10. ______________________ ☐
11. ______________________ ☐
12. ______________________ ☐
13. ______________________ ☐
14. ______________________ ☐
15. ______________________ ☐
16. ______________________ ☐
17. ______________________ ☐
18. ______________________ ☐
19. ______________________ ☐
20. ______________________ ☐

| ā | âr | är | er | ē | ēr | ī | ō | ŏŏ | ôr | ow | oy | ū | zh | ə |
|---|---|---|---|---|---|---|---|---|---|---|---|---|---|---|
| day | air | far | her | bee | tear | light | rope | book | for | cow | boy | tune | vision | item |

# Lesson 26

| | | | |
|---|---|---|---|
| 1. | ni ker o gwə | Nicaragua | Ni$^{2}$ ca$^{2}$ ra$^{2}$ gua$^{3}$ |
| 2. | mə no gwə | Managua | Ma$^{2}$ na$^{2}$ gua$^{3}$ |
| 3. | kō stə rē kə | Costa Rica | Co$^{2}$ sta$^{3}$ Ri$^{2}$ ca$^{2}$ |
| 4. | san hō sā | San Jose | San$^{3}$ Jo$^{2}$ se$^{2}$ |
| 5. | pa nə mo | Panama<br>The Capital is Panama City | Pa$^{2}$ na$^{2}$ ma$^{2}$ |
| 6. | tō dl | total | to$^{2}$ tal$^{3}$ |
| 7. | pro fit (money) | profit | prof$^{4}$ it$^{2}$ |
| 8. | pro fit (tells future) | prophet | proph$^{5}$ et$^{2}$ |
| 9. | rād | raid | raid$^{4}$ |
| 10. | vik təm | victim | vic$^{3}$ tim$^{3}$ |
| 11. | in flikt | inflict | in$^{2}$ flict$^{5}$ |
| 12. | im per fek shn | imperfection | im$^{2}$ per$^{3}$ fec$^{3}$ tion$^{4}$ |
| 13. | rī fl | rifle | ri$^{2}$ fle$^{3}$ |
| 14. | rī vl | rival | ri$^{2}$ val$^{3}$ |
| 15. | fik shn | fiction | fic$^{3}$ tion$^{4}$ |
| 16. | | | |
| 17. | | | |
| 18. | | | |
| 19. | | | |
| 20. | | | |

| ā | âr | är | er | ē | ēr | ī | ō | ŏŏ | ôr | ow | oy | ū | zh | ə |
|---|---|---|---|---|---|---|---|---|---|---|---|---|---|---|
| day | air | far | her | bee | tear | light | rope | book | for | cow | boy | tune | vision | item |

| Day 3 | | Day 4 | |
|---|---|---|---|
| 1. | ☐ | 1. | ☐ |
| 2. | ☐ | 2. | ☐ |
| 3. | ☐ | 3. | ☐ |
| 4. | ☐ | 4. | ☐ |
| 5. | ☐ | 5. | ☐ |
| 6. | ☐ | 6. | ☐ |
| 7. | ☐ | 7. | ☐ |
| 8. | ☐ | 8. | ☐ |
| 9. | ☐ | 9. | ☐ |
| 10. | ☐ | 10. | ☐ |
| 11. | ☐ | 11. | ☐ |
| 12. | ☐ | 12. | ☐ |
| 13. | ☐ | 13. | ☐ |
| 14. | ☐ | 14. | ☐ |
| 15. | ☐ | 15. | ☐ |
| 16. | ☐ | 16. | ☐ |
| 17. | ☐ | 17. | ☐ |
| 18. | ☐ | 18. | ☐ |
| 19. | ☐ | 19. | ☐ |
| 20. | ☐ | 20. | ☐ |

| ā | âr | är | er | ē | ēr | ī | ō | ŏŏ | ôr | ow | oy | ū | zh | ə |
|---|---|---|---|---|---|---|---|---|---|---|---|---|---|---|
| day | air | far | her | bee | tear | light | rope | book | for | cow | boy | tune | vision | item |

# Lesson 26b

| | | | |
|---|---|---|---|
| 1. | ni ker o gwə | Nicaragua | Ni$^{2}$ ca$^{2}$ ra$^{2}$ gua$^{3}$ |
| 2. | mə no gwə | Managua | Ma$^{2}$ na$^{2}$ gua$^{3}$ |
| 3. | kō stə  rē kə | Costa Rica | Co$^{2}$ sta$^{3}$  Ri$^{2}$ ca$^{2}$ |
| 4. | san  hō sā | San Jose | San$^{3}$  Jo$^{2}$ se$^{2}$ |
| 5. | pa nə mo | Panama | Pa$^{2}$ na$^{2}$ ma$^{2}$ |
| 6. | tō dl | total | to$^{2}$ tal$^{3}$ |
| 7. | pro fit (money) | profit | prof$^{4}$ it$^{2}$ |
| 8. | pro fit (tells future) | prophet | proph$^{5}$ et$^{2}$ |
| 9. | rād | raid | raid$^{4}$ |
| 10. | vik təm | victim | vic$^{3}$ tim$^{3}$ |
| 11. | in flikt | inflict | in$^{2}$ flict$^{5}$ |
| 12. | im per fek shn | imperfection | im$^{2}$ per$^{3}$ fec$^{3}$ tion$^{4}$ |
| 13. | rī  fl | rifle | ri$^{2}$ fle$^{3}$ |
| 14. | rī  vl | rival | ri$^{2}$ val$^{3}$ |
| 15. | fik shn | fiction | fic$^{3}$ tion$^{4}$ |
| 16. | | | |
| 17. | | | |
| 18. | | | |
| 19. | | | |
| 20. | | | |

| ā | âr | är | er | ē | ēr | ī | ō | ŏŏ | ôr | ow | oy | ū | zh | ə |
|---|---|---|---|---|---|---|---|---|---|---|---|---|---|---|
| day | air | far | her | bee | tear | light | rope | book | for | cow | boy | tune | vision | item |

## Day 1

1. ____________________ ☐
2. ____________________ ☐
3. ____________________ ☐
4. ____________________ ☐
5. ____________________ ☐
6. ____________________ ☐
7. ____________________ ☐
8. ____________________ ☐
9. ____________________ ☐
10. ____________________ ☐
11. ____________________ ☐
12. ____________________ ☐
13. ____________________ ☐
14. ____________________ ☐
15. ____________________ ☐
16. ____________________ ☐
17. ____________________ ☐
18. ____________________ ☐
19. ____________________ ☐
20. ____________________ ☐

## Day 2

1. ____________________ ☐
2. ____________________ ☐
3. ____________________ ☐
4. ____________________ ☐
5. ____________________ ☐
6. ____________________ ☐
7. ____________________ ☐
8. ____________________ ☐
9. ____________________ ☐
10. ____________________ ☐
11. ____________________ ☐
12. ____________________ ☐
13. ____________________ ☐
14. ____________________ ☐
15. ____________________ ☐
16. ____________________ ☐
17. ____________________ ☐
18. ____________________ ☐
19. ____________________ ☐
20. ____________________ ☐

| **ā** | **âr** | **är** | **er** | **ē** | **ēr** | **ī** | **ō** | **ŏŏ** | **ôr** | **ow** | **oy** | **ū** | **zh** | **ə** |
|---|---|---|---|---|---|---|---|---|---|---|---|---|---|---|
| day | air | far | her | bee | tear | light | rope | book | for | cow | boy | tune | vision | item |

# Lesson 27

| | | | | |
|---|---|---|---|---|
| 1. | kə lum bē ə | Columbia | Co$^{2}$ lum$^{3}$ bi$^{2}$ a$^{1}$ | |
| 2. | bō gə to | Bogota | Bo$^{2}$ go$^{2}$ ta$^{2}$ | |
| 3. | ven ə zwā lə | Venezuela | Ven$^{3}$ e$^{1}$ zue$^{3}$ la$^{2}$ | |
| 4. | kə ro kəs | Caracas | Car$^{3}$ a$^{1}$ cas$^{3}$ | |
| 5. | poz | pause | pause$^{5}$ | |
| 6. | rī chəs | righteous | right$^{5}$ eous$^{4}$ | T |
| 7. | ē vl | evil | e$^{1}$ vil$^{3}$ | |
| 8. | kus tə mer | customer | cus$^{3}$ tom$^{3}$ er$^{2}$ | |
| 9. | per chəs | purchase | pur$^{3}$ chase$^{5}$ | |
| 10. | tra fik | traffic | traf$^{4}$ fic$^{3}$ | |
| 11. | ol rīt | all right | all$^{3}$ right$^{5}$ | 2 Words |
| 12. | bā ker ē | bakery | ba$^{2}$ ker$^{3}$ y$^{1}$ | |
| 13. | rā vin | raven | ra$^{2}$ ven$^{3}$ | |
| 14. | fôr go tn | forgotten | for$^{3}$ got$^{3}$ ten$^{3}$ | K |
| 15. | tū ge ther | together | to$^{2}$ ge$^{2}$ ther$^{4}$ | |
| 16. | | | | |
| 17. | | | | |
| 18. | | | | |
| 19. | | | | |
| 20. | | | | |

| ā | âr | är | er | ē | ēr | ī | ō | ŏŏ | ôr | ow | oy | ū | zh | ə |
|---|---|---|---|---|---|---|---|---|---|---|---|---|---|---|
| day | air | far | her | bee | tear | light | rope | book | for | cow | boy | tune | vision | item |

## Day 3

1. ______________________ ☐
2. ______________________ ☐
3. ______________________ ☐
4. ______________________ ☐
5. ______________________ ☐
6. ______________________ ☐
7. ______________________ ☐
8. ______________________ ☐
9. ______________________ ☐
10. ______________________ ☐
11. ______________________ ☐
12. ______________________ ☐
13. ______________________ ☐
14. ______________________ ☐
15. ______________________ ☐
16. ______________________ ☐
17. ______________________ ☐
18. ______________________ ☐
19. ______________________ ☐
20. ______________________ ☐

## Day 4

1. ______________________ ☐
2. ______________________ ☐
3. ______________________ ☐
4. ______________________ ☐
5. ______________________ ☐
6. ______________________ ☐
7. ______________________ ☐
8. ______________________ ☐
9. ______________________ ☐
10. ______________________ ☐
11. ______________________ ☐
12. ______________________ ☐
13. ______________________ ☐
14. ______________________ ☐
15. ______________________ ☐
16. ______________________ ☐
17. ______________________ ☐
18. ______________________ ☐
19. ______________________ ☐
20. ______________________ ☐

| ā | âr | är | er | ē | ēr | ī | ō | ŏŏ | ôr | ow | oy | ū | zh | ə |
|---|---|---|---|---|---|---|---|---|---|---|---|---|---|---|
| day | air | far | her | bee | tear | light | rope | book | for | cow | boy | tune | vision | item |

# Lesson 27b

| | | | |
|---|---|---|---|
| 1. | kə lum bē ə | Columbia | Co$^{2}$ lum$^{3}$ bi$^{2}$ a$^{1}$ |
| 2. | bō gə to | Bogota | Bo$^{2}$ go$^{2}$ ta$^{2}$ |
| 3. | ven ə zwā lə | Venezuela | Ven$^{3}$ e$^{1}$ zue$^{3}$ la$^{2}$ |
| 4. | kə ro kəs | Caracas | Car$^{3}$ a$^{1}$ cas$^{3}$ |
| 5. | poz | pause | pause$^{5}$ |
| 6. | rī chəs | righteous | right$^{5}$ eous$^{4}$ |
| 7. | ē vl | evil | e$^{1}$ vil$^{3}$ |
| 8. | kus tə mer | customer | cus$^{3}$ tom$^{3}$ er$^{2}$ |
| 9. | per chəs | purchase | pur$^{3}$ chase$^{5}$ |
| 10. | tra fik | traffic | traf$^{4}$ fic$^{3}$ |
| 11. | ol rīt | all right | all$^{3}$ right$^{5}$ |
| 12. | bā ker ē | bakery | ba$^{2}$ ker$^{3}$ y$^{1}$ |
| 13. | rā vin | raven | ra$^{2}$ ven$^{3}$ |
| 14. | fôr go tn | forgotten | for$^{3}$ got$^{3}$ ten$^{3}$ |
| 15. | tū ge ther | together | to$^{2}$ ge$^{2}$ ther$^{4}$ |
| 16. | | | |
| 17. | | | |
| 18. | | | |
| 19. | | | |
| 20. | | | |

| ā | âr | är | er | ē | ēr | ī | ō | ŏŏ | ôr | ow | oy | ū | zh | ə |
|---|---|---|---|---|---|---|---|---|---|---|---|---|---|---|
| day | air | far | her | bee | tear | light | rope | book | for | cow | boy | tune | vision | item |

*Syllable Savvy Spelling Six*

| Day 1 | | Day 2 | |
|---|---|---|---|
| 1. | ☐ | 1. | ☐ |
| 2. | ☐ | 2. | ☐ |
| 3. | ☐ | 3. | ☐ |
| 4. | ☐ | 4. | ☐ |
| 5. | ☐ | 5. | ☐ |
| 6. | ☐ | 6. | ☐ |
| 7. | ☐ | 7. | ☐ |
| 8. | ☐ | 8. | ☐ |
| 9. | ☐ | 9. | ☐ |
| 10. | ☐ | 10. | ☐ |
| 11. | ☐ | 11. | ☐ |
| 12. | ☐ | 12. | ☐ |
| 13. | ☐ | 13. | ☐ |
| 14. | ☐ | 14. | ☐ |
| 15. | ☐ | 15. | ☐ |
| 16. | ☐ | 16. | ☐ |
| 17. | ☐ | 17. | ☐ |
| 18. | ☐ | 18. | ☐ |
| 19. | ☐ | 19. | ☐ |
| 20. | ☐ | 20. | ☐ |

| ā | âr | är | er | ē | ēr | ī | ō | ŏŏ | ôr | ow | oy | ū | zh | ə |
|---|---|---|---|---|---|---|---|---|---|---|---|---|---|---|
| day | air | far | her | bee | tear | light | rope | book | for | cow | boy | tune | vision | item |

# Lesson 28

| | | | | |
|---|---|---|---|---|
| 1. | ek wə dôr | Ecuador | Ec$^{2}$ ua$^{2}$ dor$^{3}$ | |
| 2. | kē tō | Quito | Qui$^{3}$ to$^{2}$ | |
| 3. | per ū | Peru | Pe$^{2}$ ru$^{2}$ | |
| 4. | lē mə | Lima | Li$^{2}$ ma$^{2}$ | |
| 5. | mə shēn | machine | ma$^{2}$ chine$^{5}$ | |
| 6. | ə pol ə gīz | apologize | a$^{1}$ po$^{2}$ lo$^{2}$ gize$^{4}$ | |
| 7. | not (tie) | knot | knot$^{4}$ | |
| 8. | not (nothing) | nought | nought$^{6}$ | O |
| 9. | rūt | route | route$^{5}$ | |
| 10. | kən struk shn | construction | con$^{3}$ struc$^{5}$ tion$^{4}$ | |
| 11. | skand | scanned | scan$^{4}$ned$^{3}$ | K |
| 12. | sen ter | center | cen$^{3}$ ter$^{3}$ | |
| 13. | sen trl | central | cen$^{3}$ tral$^{4}$ | |
| 14. | trē tid | treated | trea$^{4}$ ted$^{3}$ | J |
| 15. | rins | rinse | rinse$^{5}$ | |
| 16. | | | | |
| 17. | | | | |
| 18. | | | | |
| 19. | | | | |
| 20. | | | | |

| ā | âr | är | er | ē | ēr | ī | ō | ŏŏ | ôr | ow | oy | ū | zh | ə |
|---|---|---|---|---|---|---|---|---|---|---|---|---|---|---|
| day | air | far | her | bee | tear | light | rope | book | for | cow | boy | tune | vision | item |

*Syllable Savvy Spelling Six*

## Day 3

1. ____________________ ☐
2. ____________________ ☐
3. ____________________ ☐
4. ____________________ ☐
5. ____________________ ☐
6. ____________________ ☐
7. ____________________ ☐
8. ____________________ ☐
9. ____________________ ☐
10. ____________________ ☐
11. ____________________ ☐
12. ____________________ ☐
13. ____________________ ☐
14. ____________________ ☐
15. ____________________ ☐
16. ____________________ ☐
17. ____________________ ☐
18. ____________________ ☐
19. ____________________ ☐
20. ____________________ ☐

## Day 4

1. ____________________ ☐
2. ____________________ ☐
3. ____________________ ☐
4. ____________________ ☐
5. ____________________ ☐
6. ____________________ ☐
7. ____________________ ☐
8. ____________________ ☐
9. ____________________ ☐
10. ____________________ ☐
11. ____________________ ☐
12. ____________________ ☐
13. ____________________ ☐
14. ____________________ ☐
15. ____________________ ☐
16. ____________________ ☐
17. ____________________ ☐
18. ____________________ ☐
19. ____________________ ☐
20. ____________________ ☐

| ā | âr | är | er | ē | ēr | ī | ō | ŏŏ | ôr | ow | oy | ū | zh | ə |
|---|---|---|---|---|---|---|---|---|---|---|---|---|---|---|
| day | air | far | her | bee | tear | light | rope | book | for | cow | boy | tune | vision | item |

# Lesson 28b

| | | | |
|---|---|---|---|
| 1. | ek wə dôr | Ecuador | Ec$^{2}$ ua$^{2}$ dor$^{3}$ |
| 2. | kē tō | Quito | Qui$^{3}$ to$^{2}$ |
| 3. | per ū | Peru | Pe$^{2}$ ru$^{2}$ |
| 4. | lē mə | Lima | Li$^{2}$ ma$^{2}$ |
| 5. | mə shēn | machine | ma$^{2}$ chine$^{5}$ |
| 6. | ə pol ə gīz | apologize | a$^{1}$ po$^{2}$ lo$^{2}$ gize$^{4}$ |
| 7. | not (tie) | knot | knot$^{4}$ |
| 8. | not (nothing) | nought | nought$^{6}$ |
| 9. | rūt | route | route$^{5}$ |
| 10. | kən struk shn | construction | con$^{3}$ struc$^{5}$ tion$^{4}$ |
| 11. | skand | scanned | scan$^{4}$ned$^{3}$ |
| 12. | sen ter | center | cen$^{3}$ ter$^{3}$ |
| 13. | sen trl | central | cen$^{3}$ tral$^{4}$ |
| 14. | trē tid | treated | trea$^{4}$ ted$^{3}$ |
| 15. | rins | rinse | rinse$^{5}$ |
| 16. | | | |
| 17. | | | |
| 18. | | | |
| 19. | | | |
| 20. | | | |

| ā | âr | är | er | ē | ēr | ī | ō | ŏŏ | ôr | ow | oy | ū | zh | ə |
|---|---|---|---|---|---|---|---|---|---|---|---|---|---|---|
| day | air | far | her | bee | tear | light | rope | book | for | cow | boy | tune | vision | item |

## Day 1

1. ______________________ ☐
2. ______________________ ☐
3. ______________________ ☐
4. ______________________ ☐
5. ______________________ ☐
6. ______________________ ☐
7. ______________________ ☐
8. ______________________ ☐
9. ______________________ ☐
10. ______________________ ☐
11. ______________________ ☐
12. ______________________ ☐
13. ______________________ ☐
14. ______________________ ☐
15. ______________________ ☐
16. ______________________ ☐
17. ______________________ ☐
18. ______________________ ☐
19. ______________________ ☐
20. ______________________ ☐

## Day 2

1. ______________________ ☐
2. ______________________ ☐
3. ______________________ ☐
4. ______________________ ☐
5. ______________________ ☐
6. ______________________ ☐
7. ______________________ ☐
8. ______________________ ☐
9. ______________________ ☐
10. ______________________ ☐
11. ______________________ ☐
12. ______________________ ☐
13. ______________________ ☐
14. ______________________ ☐
15. ______________________ ☐
16. ______________________ ☐
17. ______________________ ☐
18. ______________________ ☐
19. ______________________ ☐
20. ______________________ ☐

| **ā** | **âr** | **är** | **er** | **ē** | **ēr** | **ī** | **ō** | **o͝o** | **ôr** | **ow** | **oy** | **ū** | **zh** | **ə** |
|---|---|---|---|---|---|---|---|---|---|---|---|---|---|---|
| day | air | far | her | bee | tear | light | rope | book | for | cow | boy | tune | vision | item |

# Lesson 29

| | | | | |
|---|---|---|---|---|
| 1. | brə zil | Brazil | Bra$^3$ zil$^3$ | |
| 2. | brə zil ē ə | Brasilia | Bra$^3$ sil$^3$ i$^1$ a$^1$ | |
| 3. | bəl i vē ə | Bolivia | Bol$^3$ i$^1$ vi$^2$ a$^1$ | |
| 4. | lə poz | La Paz | La$^2$ Paz$^3$ | |
| 5. | fas in | fasten | fast$^4$ en$^2$ | |
| 6. | kred it | credit | cred$^4$ it$^2$ | L |
| 7. | his tôr i kl | historical | his$^3$ tor$^3$ i$^1$ cal$^3$ | |
| 8. | kə nū | canoe | ca$^2$ noe$^3$ | |
| 9. | kī yak | kayak | kay$^3$ ak$^2$ | |
| 10. | sē krit | secret | se$^2$ cret$^4$ | |
| 11. | se krə târ ē | secretary | sec$^3$ re$^2$ tar$^3$ y$^1$ | |
| 12. | hoyst | hoist | hoist$^5$ | |
| 13. | chēf | chief | chief$^5$ | S |
| 14. | pēr ē əd | period | per$^3$ i$^1$ od$^2$ | |
| 15. | hēr ōz | heroes | her$^3$ oes$^3$ | |
| 16. | | | | |
| 17. | | | | |
| 18. | | | | |
| 19. | | | | |
| 20. | | | | |

| ā | âr | är | er | ē | ēr | ī | ō | ŏŏ | ôr | ow | oy | ū | zh | ə |
|---|---|---|---|---|---|---|---|---|---|---|---|---|---|---|
| day | air | far | her | bee | tear | light | rope | book | for | cow | boy | tune | vision | item |

*Syllable Savvy Spelling Six*

| Day 3 | | Day 4 | |
|---|---|---|---|
| 1. ______________ | ☐ | 1. ______________ | ☐ |
| 2. ______________ | ☐ | 2. ______________ | ☐ |
| 3. ______________ | ☐ | 3. ______________ | ☐ |
| 4. ______________ | ☐ | 4. ______________ | ☐ |
| 5. ______________ | ☐ | 5. ______________ | ☐ |
| 6. ______________ | ☐ | 6. ______________ | ☐ |
| 7. ______________ | ☐ | 7. ______________ | ☐ |
| 8. ______________ | ☐ | 8. ______________ | ☐ |
| 9. ______________ | ☐ | 9. ______________ | ☐ |
| 10. ______________ | ☐ | 10. ______________ | ☐ |
| 11. ______________ | ☐ | 11. ______________ | ☐ |
| 12. ______________ | ☐ | 12. ______________ | ☐ |
| 13. ______________ | ☐ | 13. ______________ | ☐ |
| 14. ______________ | ☐ | 14. ______________ | ☐ |
| 15. ______________ | ☐ | 15. ______________ | ☐ |
| 16. ______________ | ☐ | 16. ______________ | ☐ |
| 17. ______________ | ☐ | 17. ______________ | ☐ |
| 18. ______________ | ☐ | 18. ______________ | ☐ |
| 19. ______________ | ☐ | 19. ______________ | ☐ |
| 20. ______________ | ☐ | 20. ______________ | ☐ |

| **ā** | **âr** | **är** | **er** | **ē** | **ēr** | **ī** | **ō** | **ŏŏ** | **ôr** | **ow** | **oy** | **ū** | **zh** | **ə** |
|---|---|---|---|---|---|---|---|---|---|---|---|---|---|---|
| day | air | far | her | bee | tear | light | rope | book | for | cow | boy | tune | vision | item |

# Lesson 29b

| | | | |
|---|---|---|---|
| 1. | brə zil | Brazil | Bra$^{3}$ zil$^{3}$ |
| 2. | brə zil ē ə | Brasilia | Bra$^{3}$ sil$^{3}$ i$^{1}$ a$^{1}$ |
| 3. | bəl i vē ə | Bolivia | Bol$^{3}$ i$^{1}$ vi$^{2}$ a$^{1}$ |
| 4. | lə poz | La Paz | La$^{2}$ Paz$^{3}$ |
| 5. | fas in | fasten | fast$^{4}$ en$^{2}$ |
| 6. | kred it | credit | cred$^{4}$ it$^{2}$ |
| 7. | his tôr i kl | historical | his$^{3}$ tor$^{3}$ i$^{1}$ cal$^{3}$ |
| 8. | kə nū | canoe | ca$^{2}$ noe$^{3}$ |
| 9. | kī yak | kayak | kay$^{3}$ ak$^{2}$ |
| 10. | sē krit | secret | se$^{2}$ cret$^{4}$ |
| 11. | se krə târ ē | secretary | sec$^{3}$ re$^{2}$ tar$^{3}$ y$^{1}$ |
| 12. | hoyst | hoist | hoist$^{5}$ |
| 13. | chēf | chief | chief$^{5}$ |
| 14. | pēr ē əd | period | per$^{3}$ i$^{1}$ od$^{2}$ |
| 15. | hēr ōz | heroes | her$^{3}$ oes$^{3}$ |
| 16. | | | |
| 17. | | | |
| 18. | | | |
| 19. | | | |
| 20. | | | |

| ā | âr | är | er | ē | ēr | ī | ō | ŏŏ | ôr | ow | oy | ū | zh | ə |
|---|---|---|---|---|---|---|---|---|---|---|---|---|---|---|
| day | air | far | her | bee | tear | light | rope | book | for | cow | boy | tune | vision | item |

Syllable Savvy Spelling Six

## Day 1

1. ______ ☐
2. ______ ☐
3. ______ ☐
4. ______ ☐
5. ______ ☐
6. ______ ☐
7. ______ ☐
8. ______ ☐
9. ______ ☐
10. ______ ☐
11. ______ ☐
12. ______ ☐
13. ______ ☐
14. ______ ☐
15. ______ ☐
16. ______ ☐
17. ______ ☐
18. ______ ☐
19. ______ ☐
20. ______ ☐

## Day 2

1. ______ ☐
2. ______ ☐
3. ______ ☐
4. ______ ☐
5. ______ ☐
6. ______ ☐
7. ______ ☐
8. ______ ☐
9. ______ ☐
10. ______ ☐
11. ______ ☐
12. ______ ☐
13. ______ ☐
14. ______ ☐
15. ______ ☐
16. ______ ☐
17. ______ ☐
18. ______ ☐
19. ______ ☐
20. ______ ☐

| ā | âr | är | er | ē | ēr | ī | ō | ŏŏ | ôr | ow | oy | ū | zh | ə |
|---|---|---|---|---|---|---|---|---|---|---|---|---|---|---|
| day | air | far | her | bee | tear | light | rope | book | for | cow | boy | tune | vision | item |

# Lesson 30

| | | | | |
|---|---|---|---|---|
| 1. | chil ē | Chili | Chil$^{4}$ i$^{1}$ | M |
| 2. | san tē o gō | Santiago | San$^{3}$ ti$^{2}$ a$^{1}$ go$^{2}$ | M |
| 3. | är jin tēn ə | Argentina | Ar$^{2}$ gen$^{3}$ tin$^{3}$ a$^{1}$ | |
| 4. | yer ə von | Yerevan | Yer$^{3}$ e$^{1}$ van$^{3}$ | |
| 5. | kəm plēt lē | completely | com$^{3}$ plete$^{5}$ ly$^{2}$ | |
| 6. | fēld | field | fi$^{2}$eld$^{3}$ | |
| 7. | fer ther | further | fur$^{3}$ ther$^{4}$ | |
| 8. | fär ther | farther | far$^{3}$ ther$^{4}$ | |
| 9. | ge dēn | getting | get$^{3}$ ting$^{4}$ | K |
| 10. | in sted | instead | in$^{2}$ stead$^{5}$ | |
| 11. | sə spi shn | suspicion | su$^{2}$ spi$^{3}$ cion$^{4}$ | T |
| 12. | sə spi shs | suspicious | su$^{2}$ spi$^{3}$ cious$^{5}$ | T |
| 13. | əd mit tid | admitted | ad$^{2}$ mit$^{3}$ ted$^{3}$ | K |
| 14. | ə prōch | approach | ap$^{2}$ proach$^{6}$ | |
| 15. | vik ter ē | victory | vic$^{3}$ tor$^{3}$ y$^{1}$ | |
| 16. | | | | |
| 17. | | | | |
| 18. | | | | |
| 19. | | | | |
| 20. | | | | |

| ā | âr | är | er | ē | ēr | ī | ō | ŏŏ | ôr | ow | oy | ū | zh | ə |
|---|---|---|---|---|---|---|---|---|---|---|---|---|---|---|
| day | air | far | her | bee | tear | light | rope | book | for | cow | boy | tune | vision | item |

## Day 3

1. ________ ☐
2. ________ ☐
3. ________ ☐
4. ________ ☐
5. ________ ☐
6. ________ ☐
7. ________ ☐
8. ________ ☐
9. ________ ☐
10. ________ ☐
11. ________ ☐
12. ________ ☐
13. ________ ☐
14. ________ ☐
15. ________ ☐
16. ________ ☐
17. ________ ☐
18. ________ ☐
19. ________ ☐
20. ________ ☐

## Day 4

1. ________ ☐
2. ________ ☐
3. ________ ☐
4. ________ ☐
5. ________ ☐
6. ________ ☐
7. ________ ☐
8. ________ ☐
9. ________ ☐
10. ________ ☐
11. ________ ☐
12. ________ ☐
13. ________ ☐
14. ________ ☐
15. ________ ☐
16. ________ ☐
17. ________ ☐
18. ________ ☐
19. ________ ☐
20. ________ ☐

| **ā** | **âr** | **är** | **er** | **ē** | **ēr** | **ī** | **ō** | **ŏŏ** | **ôr** | **ow** | **oy** | **ū** | **zh** | **ə** |
|---|---|---|---|---|---|---|---|---|---|---|---|---|---|---|
| day | air | far | her | bee | tear | light | rope | book | for | cow | boy | tune | vision | item |

# Lesson 30b

| | | | |
|---|---|---|---|
| 1. | chil ē | Chili | Chil$^{4}$ i$^{1}$ |
| 2. | san tē o gō | Santiago | San$^{3}$ ti$^{2}$ a$^{1}$ go$^{2}$ |
| 3. | är jin tēn ə | Argentina | Ar$^{2}$ gen$^{3}$ tin$^{3}$ a$^{1}$ |
| 4. | yer ə von | Yerevan | Yer$^{3}$ e$^{1}$ van$^{3}$ |
| 5. | kəm plēt lē | completely | com$^{3}$ plete$^{5}$ ly$^{2}$ |
| 6. | fēld | field | fi$^{2}$eld$^{3}$ |
| 7. | fer ther | further | fur$^{3}$ ther$^{4}$ |
| 8. | fär ther | farther | far$^{3}$ ther$^{4}$ |
| 9. | ge dēn | getting | get$^{3}$ ting$^{4}$ |
| 10. | in sted | instead | in$^{2}$ stead$^{5}$ |
| 11. | sə spi shn | suspicion | su$^{2}$ spi$^{3}$ cion$^{4}$ |
| 12. | sə spi shs | suspicious | su$^{2}$ spi$^{3}$ cious$^{5}$ |
| 13. | əd mit tid | admitted | ad$^{2}$ mit$^{3}$ ted$^{3}$ |
| 14. | ə prōch | approach | ap$^{2}$ proach$^{6}$ |
| 15. | vik ter ē | victory | vic$^{3}$ tor$^{3}$ y$^{1}$ |
| 16. | | | |
| 17. | | | |
| 18. | | | |
| 19. | | | |
| 20. | | | |

| ā | âr | är | er | ē | ēr | ī | ō | ŏŏ | ôr | ow | oy | ū | zh | ə |
|---|---|---|---|---|---|---|---|---|---|---|---|---|---|---|
| day | air | far | her | bee | tear | light | rope | book | for | cow | boy | tune | vision | item |

# Spelling Rules

A

## Short and Long Vowels

Unless otherwise stated, use the short vowel sound in a word.

**sad bed lid box sun**

A long vowel sound is indicated with a line over the top of the vowel.

**ā ē ī ō ū**

**day bee light rope tune**

B

## The Schwa

**ə**

This symbol designates an unstressed "uh" sound. Instead of a schwa, a short u is used if the syllable is stressed.

*hum* **bəg humbug hum³ bug³**

Both have the same sound, but the short u is stressed and the schwa is unstressed.

C

## Y to I Rule

When adding "s" to a word that ends in "y" to make it plural, change the **y** to **i** and add **es**

**study studies**

D

## Silent Letters

Sometimes there is a silent letter in a word that does not make a sound. The pronunciation changed over the years but the spelling did not.

**talk**

**E**

## F to V

A word that ends in F or FE will be changed to VES to make it plural.

**knife knives**

**F**

## Add ES

Add **ES** instead of **S** to make the plural of words ending in S, SH, or CH.

**glass glasses**

**G**

## Very Different Pronunciations

The spelling and pronunciation of some words are very different. Sometimes the number of syllables is even different. It often helps to remember a unique pronunciation for these unusual words.

**separate sep ERāt**

**pronounced "sep rət" AND "sep ə rət"**

| | |
|---|---|
| **interest** | **in TER est** |
| **camera** | **cam ER ə** |
| **privilege** | **priv ə lij** |
| **business** | **biz ə nis** |
| **carriage** | **kâr ē əj** |
| **temperamental** | **tem per ə men tl** |
| **miniature** | **min E ə cher** |

H

## ING after Silent E

Drop the **E** at the end of a word when adding **ING**.

**bike** **biking**

I

## ED after Silent E

Drop the **E** at the end of a word when adding **ED or ER.**

**bike** **biked** **biker**

## ED

The past tense of most words is formed by adding ED to the end. The word may be pronounced "ed" or "d" or "t" at the end.

J

**"d"** **used**

**"ed"** **headed**

**"t"** **clapped**

Note that some of these words are pronounced as a single syllable. We have removed the space in the third column to show one syllable.

**clapt** **clapped** **clap$^{4}$ped$^{3}$**

## Double Consonant

Double the consonant when adding an ending with these 3 conditions

1. Word ends with a single consonant (*hop; not hope or hurt*)
2. The letter before the consonant is a single vowel (*hop; not meat*)
3. The ending begins with a vowel (*ed or ing; not hops*)

**hopping** **hopped**

L

## Open and Closed Syllables

A syllable with a short vowel sound is usually closed by a consonant at the end. A syllable with a long vowel sound is usually open with the vowel at the end of the syllable.

| | | |
|---|---|---|
| **tā bl** | **table** | **ta² ble³** |
| **ta blit** | **tablet** | **tab³ let³** |

In the word "tablet," the "b" is usually pronounced with the second syllable and not the first. However, since the "a" is a short vowel sound, it is closed with the "b" at the end of the syllable. This rule will assist in learning the spellings of many larger words.

M

## "I" makes Long "E" Sound

Some words from other countries have an "I" that says "E."

**radio**

N

## IGH

Long I sound

**high** **light** **bright**

O

## OUGH

Can make the sound of **o** or **ō** or **ū**

**thought** **though** **through**

P

## AUGH

Can make the sound of **o** or **a**

**taught** **caught** **haughty** **naughty**

**laugh**

Q

## OR

Some careers end in **OR** instead of ER.

**doctor** **sailor** **pastor**

*Draw a picture:* *"Rub-A-Dub-Dub some men in a tub and their name ends in OR"*

R

## AR

There are a limited number of words with "ar" at the end with the "er" sound.

**sugar** **pillar** **nuclear** **molecular**

*Say This: "The wizard with a lizard walked backward through the blizzard with a dollar on his collar.*

S

## I before E *"believe"*

Except After "C" *"receive"*

Or with a long "A" as in "*neighbor*" or "*weigh*."

T

## Different Endings - Same Sound

**tion** **sion** **cian**

**tial** **cial**

**ous** **ious** **eous**

U

## Contractions

An apostrophe takes the place of a missing letter or letters.

**didn't** **they'll** **he's** **I've**

36189310R00076

Made in the USA
San Bernardino, CA
15 July 2016